ALTERNATIVE LITERATURE

A practical guide for librarians

To my parents
and
to Kate and Daniel

Alternative Literature:

A Practical Guide for Librarians

Chris Atton

Gower

#33079773

Published by
Gower Publishing Limited
Gower House
Croft Road
Aldershot
Hampshire GU11 3HR
England

Gower
Old Post Road
Brookfield
Vermont 05036
USA

British Library Cataloguing in Publication Data

Atton, Chris
  Alternative Literature: Practical Guide
  for Librarians
  I. Title
  025.21

  ISBN 0–566–07665–9

Typeset in 11/13 Palatino by Raven Typesetters, Chester and printed
in Great Britain by Hartnolls Ltd, Bodmin

Contents

Preface

For many people the publications of the alternative press are a peripheral concern, the province of the fanatic and the dilettante. There is a widespread belief that these titles are not only few in number but that they are utterly marginal to mainstream librarianship and research. Hardly at all is alternative literature considered as part of a wider picture: the dominant tendency is to marginalize both it and its creators. But to do so is to underestimate both the role and the nature of alternative literature. The quantity of titles alone published each year make it a significant part of publishing, yet few of these are noted in the mainstream media that most of us take to learn about the world. Fewer still find their way onto the shelves of bookshops and libraries. Their virtual invisibility to all but the assiduous – and well-informed – searcher ensures that their quality will be even less regarded.

There are many reasons for this. Some have to do with the inadequacy of the mass media to give a detailed enough picture of the world; others with established methods of stock selection that ignore almost all small, independent publishers. There are also our own prejudices and biases that tell us that if we do not already know about it, then it cannot be worth knowing.

Consequently, this book must serve a number of purposes. Unlike most introductions to specific types of literature, it may not assume that its readers are all equally aware of its subject matter, and that all it must do is offer pointers to information sources, without further comment. Instead it must begin by defining alternative literature and by examining the concerns and the nature of such publications that call themselves 'alternative'. In doing so it will also demonstrate the value of these publications and assess their place in a library collection, insofar as they provide coverage of subjects ignored by the mainstream, and as they offer counters to the dominant views presented in mainstream publications. It must also critically examine the ways in which we do our selection and our research, and offer other ways that complement those existing, to help us identify this alternative literature. Finally it needs to recognize that such work is not to be undertaken lightly and that anyone considering it will find the assistance of sympathetic colleagues, publishers and distributors of especial value.

In examining alternative literature from this wider perspective it will be found that it is far from marginal or minimal. Indeed, the profusion of titles and subjects covered by it are such that it is impossible to provide comprehensive coverage in a single book. Such an attempt would be as foolish as an attempt to give a similar treatment to the range of mainstream publishing. (And it is very likely that the plethora of alternative presses and their titles far exceeds that of the mainstream.) The novel nature of many alternative titles would also entail a far more detailed description and analysis than those of the mainstream: unfamiliar ideas inevitably require lengthier expositions than their better known, mainstream counterparts.

Consequently this book is more to do with a philosophy of librarianship, a way of thinking about librarianship and a way of doing librarianship that might be quite different from the methods of selection and acquisition employed by many librarians in their daily work, as different as the publications of the alternative presses are from those of the mainstream. In the course of outlining this philosophy and its methods, as wide a range of alternative literature as possible will be discussed, covering electronic sources as well as printed. This book cannot be an 'enquire within upon everything', but it can at least provide strategies and examples, help and enthusiasm to assist librarians in developing their stock to take account of this vast, yet largely ignored source of ideas and information. For despite that word 'philosophy', librarianship and research is after all about action, about praxis. Although it may not be the last word on alternative literature, at least this book might provide ideas for action.

Chris Atton

Acknowledgements

I would like to thank Will Lawson and Neil Stoddart for valuable discussions about the nature of alternative literature, and John Pateman of Hackney Libraries and Sally Kerr of Edinburgh City Libraries for their encouragement throughout the writing of the book. Sally, along with Gill Harris of LINK, also made it possible for me to present parts of this book as talks and seminars. Chris Dodge of Hennepin County Library generously provided much information and reading matter. I especially thank him for *Plunderphonics*. I am indebted to Charles Willett of CRISES Press for his example and enthusiasm, and for allowing my work a wider audience. Sanford Berman of Hennepin County Library has been a continual inspiration. I should also note the unwitting contribution made by James Danky of the State Historical Society of Wisconsin.

Pat Kennedy and Helen Matthews of Napier University Library advised me on the storage of unusual formats. Martyn Lowe of Librarians Within The Peace Movement supplied many sources of peace information. John McMillan drew my attention to John Quail's book, *The slow burning fuse*.

For their support: Brenda Loew Tatelbaum of *EIDOS*; all at *This Magazine*; Joseph A. Gervasi of *NO LONGER A FANzine*; Dean Plant at AK Press. Finally, I would like to thank all those editors and publishers who sent me copies of their publications, many of whom I know can ill afford to do so. I hope that this book adequately acknowledges their endeavours.

CA

Introduction

A little history

In the 1960s the phrase 'underground literature' was used to describe the newspapers and broadsides of the peace activists opposed to the Vietnam War; the pamphlets of the Marxist-Leninists and the followers of Mao; the underground music magazines reviewing bands not discussed in the mainstream music press; the celebration of the burgeoning drug culture; poetry chapbooks produced on kitchen tables. Many of these, such as *The Village Voice*, had remarkable longevity and went 'overground'. Others exchanged long life for notoriety, like *Oz*. Others, such as *Frendz*, quietly faded away. The ensuing decades saw the consolidation of many titles and subject areas. Somewhere along the line the underground press became the small or independent press, terms that are still current today. In some areas this meant a slow incorporation into the mainstream. The writings of the political left were for many years only published by small, independent publishers. The 1970s saw the rise of publishers such as Pluto, now established in the mainstream as the prime suppliers of such works. Indeed, the incorporation of Marxist studies into the academic curriculum has meant rich pickings for many mainstream publishers and booksellers, with the consequence that many small publishers and booksellers have found their purpose usurped. Some, like Pluto, have adapted to the commercial world with ease. Others have gone under. Still others – as we shall see – have remained fiercely independent. These political publishers are resolutely amateur, small-scale operations. They publish on a not-for-profit basis, refusing to compromise either their principles or their authors by insisting on manuscripts whose primary function is to make money. As such, they have a freedom that many commercial publishers literally cannot afford.

The world of independently produced poetry and fiction has if anything remained even further out of sight of the mainstream markets, where it has nevertheless flourished, being no less strong today than it was 30 years ago. For many the term 'small press' is synonymous with small-scale, independent literary publishing, and the term 'little magazine' is now used exclusively to describe periodicals anthologizing and reviewing such work.

Already we are coming across variant terminology. Some use terms such as small press and independent publisher interchangeably. Others still use underground to describe the more extreme forms of independent publishing: the scruffy samizdat of disaffected youth, perhaps. These terms seem to fall into two categories: the more or less neutral descriptions such as small press, independent publisher, little magazine, and emotive terms such as underground, radical, dissenting. The terms in the first category have wide, vague meanings, denoting the nature of the publishing enterprise in relation to the mainstream, commercial publishing world. The terms in the second category have more to do with the oppositional stance and the value judgements inherent in the content of the publications. From the point of view of mainstream commentators, such terms connote publications of a dangerous, even seditious nature.

Until the latter half of the 1970s, independent publishing was in fact thoroughly *dependent*: dependent on the printing technology of the time, costly and time-consuming, unless it fell back on the cheapest methods of reproduction used in offices and schools, machines like the Gestetner and the Roneo. These were at best messy, unreliable and perhaps even more time-consuming than employing professional printers. But the rise of the photocopier opened up a new avenue for cheap, quick reproduction. The photocopier was fast, clean and mostly reliable. The Punk explosion of 1976 saw for the first time dozens of music magazines published in photocopied formats, using a variety of typefaces, handwriting, often illustrated with plagiarized graphics and photographs from the music press and record sleeves. The do-it-yourself ethic of Punk music was carried over into its publications. These exuberantly dispensed with niceties such as professional layout and print runs. Many were chaotic collages, cut-ups of image and text; the number printed had more to do with what each editor (frequently the sole contributor) had in ready cash at the time. Most were probably given away. None made money, few broke even, even fewer lasted longer than a few months. However short-lived, they were able to document events far more rapidly – and, some would say, accurately – than the mainstream music press. They tended to publish whenever they had something to say; being part of their local scene they were closer to what was happening than the professional journalist from the big city. Through their ethos and their views, in their format and style, by their channels of distribution and their disregard for commercial considerations, they provided a real alternative to the mainstream versions of events and the mainstream methods of doing business.

The advent of desktop publishing in the 1980s had a further impact on the independent publishing scene. Now the ability to produce one's own camera-ready, typeset text ready for printing made short print runs for independent book publishers far more cost effective. Some publishers used photocopiers filled with high quality paper for an even cheaper, but no less professional, end product. Laser printers and fax machines have enabled the independent publishers to run their enterprise from home, with as much efficacy as they might require (short of turning commercial). In the 1990s the possibilities for electronic publishing via the Internet have been embraced by many in alternative publishing. Printing and distribution overheads, advertising and promotion budgets, all can be dispensed with.

There are many alternative methods of publishing and production, just as there have always been many alternative points of view, many alternative versions of the world, many alternative sources of information. Yet are these not already available to us through mainstream channels? It might appear that we live in a world of easily accessible, ever-increasing information and entertainment, knowledge and ideas are easily accessible, ever available. We need only look at the mushrooming of satellite television channels, radio stations, newspapers and magazines. What more could we possibly want? But even a cursory glance at the television schedules or the magazine racks will tell us that we could want much more: all we have is more of the same. Where five years ago there were a handful of computing magazines, now even the smallest newsagent stocks 20. The largest stock anything up to 100. The news, reviews and reporting in these are largely uniform. The increase in glossy music magazines has mostly meant an increase in the number of glossy photographs and unsearching interviews of this week's 'big thing'. On British newsracks at least, the range of political views available is incredibly narrow. With the exception of *The Morning Star* (a Communist daily carried by a tiny minority of newsagents) the daily newspapers and current affairs magazines inhabit the same political ground as the three main parliamentary parties. Consequently, all political debate and analysis tends to be carried within the framework of adversarial parliamentary, representative democracy. Notions such as collectivism, direct democracy, local empowerment, anarchism or libertarianism are not considered. As the ownership of the mass media continues to be concentrated into the hands of a few, so the opportunity to hear such dissenting voices is reduced. The voices of the individual, of the community, of the oppressed, of those different from others, are hardly ever heard. On the rare occasions they are heard, they are mediated and marginalized by considerations of what makes 'a good story'. They may well turn up in academic studies as the subject of a sociological investigation, but still they will not be heard in their own right.

What began as underground publishing and continues to be championed as independent from the controlling influence of commercial considerations, what began as agitational and oppositional enterprises some 30 years ago, have now become the lifeblood for many. The opportunity to make one's voice heard in the way one chooses, not in the way someone else chooses for you (a reporter, an editor, an academic): that is at the heart of alternative publishing.

Which leaves us with: what? An independent publishing scene that encompasses hardback and paperback titles and magazines from publishers of long-standing; home-produced books and pamphlets whose production values are indistinguishable from their mainstream counterparts; hand-made magazines and broadsides that could not be further from the mainstream in either their content or their format. A few of these publications you will see on the shelves of high street bookshops in cities and larger towns. Some you will see only in the cooperatively-owned radical bookshops. Most you simply will not see at all. That you will not see most of the publications referred to in this book only makes explanations of their nature more difficult.

Vaclav Havel has suggested the phrase 'parallel culture' to refer to 'nothing more and nothing less than a culture which for various reasons will not, cannot, or may not reach out to the public through the media which fall under state control'.[1] McGuff argues that by using this phrase we can free 'the alternative scene' from the straitjacket imposed upon it by the dominant culture, which takes great pains to portray it as 'a frightening avant garde', at once demonizing and marginalizing its producers and their products. McGuff sees the dominant and the parallel cultures at the opposite ends of two related scales: ease of entry into the culture and the challenge to oneself within that culture. The ease with which one can enter the parallel culture (you only need access to pen, paper and a photocopier to start publishing) has a levelling function, making it an extremely democratic culture. By contrast, entry into the dominant culture of mass publishing and mass communication is guarded by those who control the media, the printing presses, the television studios; you enter on their terms, not on your own. The second scale has to do with creativity: the parallel culture, Havel argues, encourages individual creativity, which is at a premium in the dominant culture. Again, the creative input of the individual is bounded and filtered by what the controllers of the media want to publish. As a truly independent author and publisher, on the other hand, you can say anything you like, how you like. Democracy and challenge: these principles are at the heart of this parallel culture.

What does 'alternative' include?

Given the diversity of publications, to attempt to define alternative literature concisely is not at all straightforward. The editors of *Alternatives in Print* have, however, suggested three simple criteria, by which to define alternative publishers.[2] These are worth considering as a starting point. They hold that a publisher might be thought of as alternative if it met at least one of the following:

1. The publisher has to be non-commercial, demonstrating 'a basic concern for ideas, not the concern for profit, is the motivation for publication'.
2. The subject matter of their publications should focus on 'social responsibility or creative expression, or usually a combination of both'.
3. Finally, it is enough for publishers to define themselves as alternative publishers.

The inclusive nature of these criteria raises the question: Where do we draw the line between mainstream publications and alternative (or parallel) publications? Are we to include the publications of charities and non-profit making pressure groups here? Do Greenpeace or Amnesty International therefore count as alternative publishers? If social responsibility is paramount, may we include the for-profit publications of such publishers as Pluto Press and Verso? Turning to our third criterion, if we are to admit any publisher who likes to think of themselves as 'alternative', could we not include nationally-distributed magazines such as

New Statesman and Society and *The Nation*? Some publishers, including those in the Committee of Small Magazine Editors and Publishers wish to be known as independent rather than alternative, in order to highlight 'the takeover of once large and independent publishing houses by multinational corporations... More so than ever before these self-styled independent presses reflect the unfettered freedom to publish.'[3] The self-styled independent publisher can now include the internationally-distributed hardback publisher free of conglomerate control as easily as it can the publisher of a single pamphlet with a print run of 50.

The range of alternative literature described in this book takes its defining characteristics in equal parts from Havel's notion of parallel culture and the criteria taken from *Alternatives in Print*. The inclusion and discussion of topics and titles and publishers are based on two simple questions: Are the topics or perspectives unknown or marginalised in the mainstream? Are the publishers and organizations responsible generally absent from mainstream library collections and bibliographic tools? If the answer to both questions is: 'Yes', then we shall consider it as alternative literature. This results in a broad definition of the literature, which is more useful than a more exclusive view based on political dogma, ideology, morals or similar relativistic notions. This broad definition is able to include the publications of what might be termed the 'major' alternative publishers and distributors, both the commercial independents such as Pluto, Verso and distributors such as Turnaround and Troika, as well as those non-profit making collectives such as South End Press, Common Courage and Black Rose Books. It will include literature produced by pressure groups, single-interest organizations and NGOs, except where their work is already well-known in the mainstream. The work of Greenpeace and Friends of the Earth has effectively been assimilated into the mainstream, whereas the work of Campaign Against Arms Trade and TAPOL still does not have that visibility. Finally, it will include what for many is the true alternative literature: those short-run pamphlets, magazines, tracts and rants where new ideas and information circulate in chaotic profusion in what Bob Black has called 'the marginals milieu'.

What alternative literature is not

There are two types of publishing with which alternative literature is sometimes conflated: vanity publishing and grey literature. In fact, it is neither. It is true that it does encourage self-publishing and that it is home to authors who cannot publish elsewhere, but its purpose is not to publish them at their own expense for another's gain. As amongst mainstream publishers, some alternative publishers offer contracts, whilst others make it clear that no commercial gain will accrue to the author through publication (just as in academic journal publishing). Where the two streams of publishing differ is in self-publishing, which is the forte of the alternative press; many would say it is the true alternative. Authors that publish their own work are hardly ever taken seriously by the mainstream press (although self-publishers of hobbyist and local history titles seem to be acceptable). When Timothy Mo – three times shortlisted for the Booker Prize – decided to publish his novel *Brownout of Breadfruit Boulevard* under his own imprint, the literary world was 'aghast', according to a report in *The Guardian*, at this 'unprecedented step for an established author'.[4] Yet only the previous year (1994) Jill Paton Walsh, unable to find a large commercial publisher for her novel *Knowledge of Angels*, had done precisely the same thing. Paton Walsh's novel duly appeared on the Booker Prize shortlist, and it is a measure of how self-publishing is seen by mainstream literati that this caused some disquiet. Yet there are hundreds of authors who have no wish to be 'established' who are taking the same step every year, and have been doing so for many years already. They publish their own works not simply because they cannot find a commercial home for them, but because they want to retain complete control over every stage of the publishing process. They publish not from vanity and weakness but from positions of self-confidence and independence. Yet still the mainstream media insist that self-publishing 'is a course favoured only as a desperate last resort'.

Grey literature, in common with such terms as primary sources and secondary sources, may be a useful term to those involved in collection management, but it tells us little about the nature and content of alternative literature. Within the library profession alternative literature is often considered as a part of grey literature. In terms of the ideas and views that it promulgates, alternative literature could not be more different from the company and government reports, and the occasional literature of science and technology that is normally termed 'grey literature'. But there are common features which, whilst not helpful in defining alternative literature, do at least account for some of the problems in identifying and acquiring it, such as a lack of comprehensive bibliographic control and low print runs. We shall return to these when we examine the problems of acquisition later in the book.

The scope of this book

The aim of this book is to introduce librarians, researchers and others interested in understanding and acquiring alternative literature beyond the mainstream to the immense range of knowledge and information available. The book is wholly concerned with English language publications and all the titles, publishers and distributors discussed in this book (with the exception of a handful of Canadian items) come from the UK and the US. This is no deliberate exclusion of other English-speaking countries, rather it is an index of where the author's own researches into collection development opportunities have led, although examples have been chosen that would be equally relevant for any public library or the general reader. Since the bulk of the selection tools for alternative literature (few as they are) are published in the US, they do tend to represent US (and, to a lesser degree, UK) publications.

The emphasis is on developing a collection of current materials and coming to understand such materials as a supplement and a parallel to mainstream acquisitions of libraries. Consequently, historical bibliographical works are excluded, except on the rare occasion where they illuminate the current nature and extent of alternative literature. There is an emphasis on information and strategies for the acquisition of current titles, along with advice on how to sustain and develop collections.

The book ignores what little coverage the mainstream indexes, abstracts and directories give to the alternative press, preferring to concentrate on less well-known information sources from the alternative press itself. Those 'vigorous individuals' (to borrow Charles Willett's felicitous phrase) already engaged in the selection of alternative literature will no doubt be familiar with much of what is here – but even they should find something new here. (Some of those people produce their own review and discussion journals, newsletters and books. The reader will find mention of their endeavours in Chapter 6.)

It is not only the tools, the titles and the publishers that will be unfamiliar to many readers. The subject matter of much alternative literature will also be new. Essential to understanding the alternative press is an introduction to its dominant themes. As much as it is possible to reduce thousands of viewpoints into a handful of topics, this book provides introductions to these topics, aiming to define them as well as indicate their importance.

It is impossible, however, to enumerate all the subjects covered by alternative literature, just as it would be to enumerate all the subjects covered by mainstream literature. Even merely to list them would be an extremely lengthy task, little would be gained by it and such a list would not in itself aid our understanding of alternative literature. It would also be impossible to cover all titles published by the alternative press. Such a task would in fact be worthless, since it would have the opposite effect of what is introduced here: their very prolificness would confuse and discourage people from investigating them further.

Another way would be to take a generalist approach: looking at the rough contours of the literature, its common characteristics, its nature and extent; examining questions of availability and bibliographic control. But this approach runs the risk of focusing too much on the nature of the publications as documents for storage and retrieval, ignoring their cultural and social value. Such an approach would give little indication of how such literature can supplement a collection of mainstream literature;

rather it would focus on the problematic nature of alternative literature at the expense of its advantages.

This book aims to provide a middle way which, by the use of case studies of specific subject areas, will give concrete examples of the nature and extent of the literature. It will also look in detail at the most appropriate bibliographic tools and strategies for keeping up to date in this continually changing field of publishing. Although change is hardly unique to alternative publishing, the lack of many formal methods of bibliographic control means that the librarian and researcher exploring this field must look further than the standard tools such as bibliographies and indexes, relying as much on networking through the literature itself, as well as through like-minded organizations and individuals. In common with many alternative publishing endeavours, even these more unconventional sources might have short lives or change their nature precipitously. Rare indeed is the alternative bibliographic source of constancy and long standing. The life of a small, independent publisher is a precarious one and there is no guarantee that what exists today will still be there tomorrow. Tomorrow there might be a new publisher covering the field more comprehensively; new fields of study might easily arise. This continual flux has made choosing representative titles and publishers difficult; some that may well not exist by the time you read this. Consider them as examples; you'll be able to replace them with examples of your own in the future.

But it is important to be able to provide a flavour of the nature of titles available, along with their publishers and distributors. The examples in this book have therefore been chosen according to the following criteria:

1. Their relevance in the subject area – each title or publisher should be representative of either a broad subject area, a number of topics or be the primary or a distinct source of information on a topic.
2. Their value to the librarian or researcher – each title should be of potential use to the librarian, not only as it provides information on its subject, but as it provides the opportunity to learn more about the topic at hand through its provision of

bibliographies, references, reviews and its value as a networking tool.

The first chapter of this book looks at the general characteristics of alternative literature, its most prominent features and some of the publishing forms it has developed. The dominant themes of alternative literature are examined in the second chapter of the book, but such is the importance of alternative literature as a counter to the mass media, however, that this topic is treated in detail in Chapter 3. A proper understanding of the role and value of alternative literature must also entail an appreciation of how the mainstream media, mainstream publishing and, regrettably, mainstream library provision have together prevented the views and ideas expressed in the alternative press from being heard. So these chapters are followed by an examination of the problems facing librarians and researchers who want to find out more about alternative literature. Reasons are explored for the general absence of alternative literature from mainstream sources of information, including bookshops, libraries and bibliographic sources. There then follows a discussion of how these problems might be solved and an examination of the general sources that are available for identifying and selecting alternative literature. A separate chapter looks at various current awareness strategies that might be employed for keeping abreast of this extremely fluid field of publishing. The final chapter deals with the challenges that alternative literature brings to libraries and information units in terms of publicity, cataloguing and classification and methods of storage. Full details of all titles, publishers, distributors and organizations mentioned in the text are gathered together at the end of the book. Here are described the more successful methods by which alternative literature might best be incorporated into the stock of any library, with a resulting improvement in the technical aspects of stock acquisition and retrieval. But, above all, the greatest impact alternative literature can have lies in the benefits to the users by having at their disposal a library that comprehensively encompasses the wealth of knowledge, ideas, opinions and information of contemporary society.

References

1. Quoted by Luke McGuff in 'Parallel Culture', *CVS Bulletin*, First Dispatch, February 1993, 1822–5.
2. *Alternatives in print: an international catalog of books, pamphlets, periodicals and audiovisual materials*, compiled by the Task Force on Alternatives in Print, Social Responsibilities Round Table, American Library Association, Sixth edition (New York, NY: Neal-Schuman; London: Mansell; 1980), vii.
3. Ibid.
4. John Mullin, 'Timothy Mo sets up shop as his own publisher', *The Guardian*, 25 February 1995, p. 2.

1 The Nature and Value of Alternative Literature

Although we have noted a few examples of the topics that alternative literature covers, we have not yet addressed the broad questions: What is alternative literature about? What are its concerns? To answer these precisely would be to ascribe to the literature a homogeneity it simply does not possess. Just as there are a multiplicity of formats, a variety of publishers operating in a variety of ways, there are also thousands of authors and editors who have entered the world of alternative publishing to make their own voice heard, to give their version of events, to provide information and knowledge that may very well be unique to them. However it is possible to identify a number of features, the dominant intellectual characteristics, if you will, of alternative literature, that either singly or together typify its immense output.

Firstly, alternative literature offers critiques of mainstream themes and perspectives that provide thoroughgoing analyses of the media's representation of business and government interests. An example of this is the continuing human rights abuses by Indonesia. Here the dominant view, although it acknowledges Indonesia's victims, nevertheless focuses on that country's geopolitical role as a major player in the opening of markets to the West in the Asia-Pacific area. Insofar as it sustains the mass media through generating advertising revenue, critical represent-ations of business and commerce in the mass media tend to be spasmodic and shallow. Free from such constraints, the alterna-tive media are able to research and publish aspects of business practices not covered elsewhere.

But alternative literature goes further than critical discussion and proposes alternative value systems to put in the place of those of the mainstream. It also suggests methods for educating and organizing, for developing activism in all aspects of our life. It provides not simply different ways of looking at the world, but ways of changing the world. Such calls to action are especially valuable in a culture where we are increasingly encouraged to be passive spectators of world events, where communities have been replaced by isolated units linked not socially but electroni-cally, through the television, telephone and modem. Rebuilding those communities and empowering people within those com-munities are two of the tasks of alternative literature.

The novel nature of much that is published here should not be forgotten. Many subjects are unique to alternative literature: it is the only source for such information. Some of these subjects do in time become assimilated into the mainstream: environmental and human rights activists first found a home for their writings in the alternative press. Themes and perspectives that act as counters to the themes of mainstream literature are also to be found: the peace movement is hardly represented at all in the mass media. During the Gulf War the emphasis was on high-tech warfare and tactics, where euphemisms such as 'collateral dam-age' and 'surgical strike' disguised the real nature and scale of the attacks on Iraq. The pacifist version of events was never heard beyond the alternative press. At present, the majority of anarchist and situationist works is published by the alternative press.

If there is a single force behind all these characteristics it is the necessity for social change. This can mean anything from chal-lenging conventional notions of who may be considered an artist or a social commentator, to wholesale programmes for political and economic revolution, and all points imaginable between the two. But let us not confuse social change with party politics. Only a small proportion of alternative literature is taken up with political debate of the kinds familiar to us from the mainstream media. Party political issues are hardly ever to be found here. What is it then that sets such publications apart from the 'political'? To answer this we need to examine the notion of 'social change'. The underlying notion of most alternative publications goes beyond party political activity. It also goes beyond the political activity of the more adversarial minority parties such as the Socialist Workers' Party and the Revolutionary Communist Party. Rather than attempt change within the pre-existing structures of government, alternative publications and their producers tend to discuss their subjects either in opposition to, or independently of, such structures. This is not to say that every alternative publication is necessarily promoting revolution nor that every alternative publication is necessarily seditious. It is simply that the topics are addressed outwith what is considered to be the straitjacket of unthinking, uncritical orthodoxy.

The value of alternative publications

The overriding point to make here is that since the material has been published, should it not therefore enjoy equal consideration with the publications of the mainstream? Many – probably the majority – of these publications are marginalized due to their inability to compete in the market place with the conglomerate, international publishing houses. By choosing to ignore or by remaining ignorant of such publications we cannot but disadvantage our users. By denying them even the opportunity to become aware that such literature exists we are surely failing at least those who, in the words of Maurice Line, 'browse as a means of articulating half-identified needs or simply for curiosity'.[1]

But it is in their content, inevitably, where lies the most powerful argument for their acquisition, in the extent to which they provide an alternative to the orthodoxies and doctrines of the mass media. Bypassing the mass media, in many cases forsaking commercial gain, by refusing to play by the rules of the free market, alternative publications can provide us with different perspectives on subjects, even wholly new or hitherto unknown subjects. Much investigative reporting takes place in the pages of small circulation journals, for example, *Lobster*, the British journal of parapolitics, was the first to break the story about Colin Wallace and 'Operation Clockwork Orange', the MI5 plot to destabilize the Wilson Government. Well before *The Sunday Times* and *Nature* locked horns, *Open Eye* published an annotated feature on Peter Duesberg and the AIDS/HIV controversy, which also included notes on where to find more on 'unconventional viewpoints' regarding AIDS. The US journal *CovertAction Quarterly* last year published an extensive feature on British military tactics to target Republican teenagers in Northern Ireland for harassment and even death. Three stories: two of which were not picked up the mass media until much later, and then often reported in superficial, sensationalist and partisan terms. The third, to the author's knowledge, has still gone unreported in the British press.

The value of alternative publications then lies in their providing interpretations of the world which we might not otherwise see and information about the world that we simply will not find anywhere else. It is precisely because, in Charles Willett's words, 'they are not filtered, sanitized, and packaged by the giant corporations that deliver most information we receive' that they are able to achieve this.[2] Alternative publications are at bottom more interested in the free flow of ideas than in profit. They are answerable not to accountants, but to their writers and readers.

Considering alternative publications for a library or as part of a research project therefore becomes as inevitable as the consideration presently given to the (narrow) range of mainstream publications normally found in library collections. The implications for, say, a public reference service or postgraduate research are equally important. Without access to a collection that approaches comprehensiveness the librarian or researcher can hardly pretend to have at their command a reasonably complete picture of the world, both in terms of viewpoints and mere quantity of information. The reference librarian or researcher that only makes use of periodical indexes such as *British Humanities Index* and the *British Newspapers Index* (let alone *The Times Index*) and ignores the plethora of journals, newspapers and magazines covering those events unreported by the mass media or only recounted from only one perspective (such as are featured in *Alternative Press Index* and *The Left Index*) will fail to account for those other perspectives.

Most libraries, furthermore, should also reflect the communities in which they live, reflecting the interests of the various cultures. Most libraries stock the small press titles relating to local history, but few appear to have any interest in the local publishers of other material. How many libraries, for instance, can provide information on local alternative publishers? Having such information available would of course automatically provide an index (in its non-technical sense) to the interests and nature of significant sections of the local community, interests perhaps even ignored by local bookshops. In the author's own city there are a number of alternative publishers, including one which is also a major distributor of alternative titles. Yet of three university library services and a major public library service (a total in excess of 100 separate collections) only one library in Edinburgh deals with this distributor at all. Smaller publishers are worse off. It seems that no library in Edinburgh has an interest in stocking this material as local cultural artefacts, notwithstanding their content. But should not every town and city not consider providing access to such titles, using the 'local interest' argument, even if the content is not appropriate for a particular community's needs?

Our libraries are often hosts to local creative writing, indeed many librarians actively promote writing as the necessary accompaniment to the promotion of reading. Anthologies of amateur writing will often find a natural home in the local library. Local historians may also expect their work to be acquired by the local library. But how many libraries stock other works by local authors and small publishers? Here we go beyond the informational needs of our community and examine its cultural life and its representation through publication: how many libraries in Britain, for instance, collect the fanzines of local football clubs and music fans? Libraries, in their capacity as repositories for local historical information, might well archive newspapers and the proceedings of local societies, but how many have identified and acquired the products of working-class culture, for example, the opinions and publications of ordinary people on matters that affect them daily within their immediate environment?

Many popular movements are only documented in alternative publications. Much social history and many aspects of contemporary society will be lost to us if we do not consider alternative publications as part of our libraries' collections or as part of our research. In the introduction to his *The slow burning fuse: the lost history of British anarchists,* John Quail noted that 'the sources for the Anarchist movement are extremely scattered ... even quite large circulation [anarchist] papers can only be read in sequence by following odd copies from library to library'.[3] Were more libraries to stock alternative publications systematically such research would cease to be the province of the isolated researcher, and be more accessible to the population at large, especially those to whom such history properly belongs.

The popular nature of alternative literature

It might seem odd to use the word 'popular' to describe alternative literature, since in one sense it is far from popular. Mostly it circulates amongst a small readership, the typical range being a few thousand down to a few dozen in extreme cases. It is largely unheard of outside its own circles, with a low (at times non-existent) profile in mainstream culture. It is generally absent from libraries and bookshops. Yet this should not lead us to believe that alternative literature is merely the product of a coterie, an élitist confection designed to exclude the majority of the population. On the contrary, much of it is expressly popular in that it is written by and aimed firmly at an audience of 'ordinary people'. We may well be unfamiliar with the topics its writers explore, but that does not necessarily make them recondite. Much alternative literature is the home for topics not considered elsewhere; novel subject matter should come as no surprise. (There are to be found any number of obscurantist polemicists, of course, but they are hardly peculiar to alternative literature.)

Given that much alternative literature deals with novel subject matter or is published in order to explore a subject from a hitherto unconsidered perspective, much care will often be taken to use language simply and clearly. Writers will eschew jargon and complex syntax, preferring a simple and clear exposition of topics that affect all of us, every day of our lives. This is especially true of publications and publishers that are to do with social empowerment, advocacy and education.

The titles of South End Press document the struggles against racism, sexism and environmental destruction, at the same time as they offer analyses and strategies for social change at local, national and international levels. New Society Publishers declares itself 'dedicated to promoting fundamental social change through non-violent action' and publishes books providing background essays and ideas for working together in groups and communities on non-violent resistance, as well as resources for parents and teachers. The Charles H. Kerr Publishing Company was founded in 1886 and may be considered the oldest alternative publisher in the US, yet its aim today 'remains what it always has been: to publish books that will help make this planet a good place to live!'

Some of the most lucid, readable and therefore impactful, writing on the mass media originates amongst publishers such as these. Much of what alternative literature exists to promulgate is ordinary, everyday – another irony, since people unacquainted with it often dismiss it as 'weird'. Consider those terms that we noted earlier: underground, radical, seditious. Even the Russian samizdat, when applied to publications of the West, tends to refer to a scruffy, small circulation pamphlet of scurrilous origin. It has nothing in common with its noble, Soviet dissident cousin, the shining beacon in the eternal night of an oppressed society.

The nature of alternative publishing also tends to be more egalitarian than its mainstream counterparts, based as they are on profit and utilizing highly compartmentalized, hierarchical organizations. By contrast the structure of the alternative media tends towards the collective: both in sharing resources for research and in democratizing the nature of their work. This often means that every person involved in an alternative publication has a hand (or at least a responsibility) in every part of the work. Since most alternative publications are not produced for profit but out of conviction or commitment, resources are often shared – what would be impossible for one author or even a single organization to achieve is possible through the collective or loose amalgam of individuals and organizations. We see this most vividly in the long-term critical research that takes place within the alternative media, that is a crucial role of the alternative media in any country. Such work, amongst a wide range of disparate sources – perhaps yielding no publishable results for months or even years – is ill-suited to the short-term goals of mainstream publishing.

Alternative literature – both as a mode of production and as a medium – is highly democratic. Those involved in alternative publishing are there because it gives them freedom. Perhaps they were unable to make their voices heard within mainstream publishing; perhaps their work is too critical of the mainstream to be published by the mainstream; perhaps the innovative nature of their subject matter or style of presentation is too untested in the market place for a mainstream publisher to risk. Whatever the reason, alternative publishing offers all such people an opportunity to disseminate their ideas. They are able to retain control over their work and establish their independence from the mainstream. But the means of production available to the low-budget do-it-yourself publisher often fall far short of those available to the mass publisher. The desideratum of publishing for a wide audience must often be abandoned and along with it such niceties as sophisticated design, layout, printing and binding techniques need to be replaced by whatever is cheap and available. The most primitive publications are handwritten and photocopied. A variety of styles, formats, layouts and print runs arises, far different from the standard book sizes and formats familiar from entries in *Global Books in Print*. Standards of presentation may count for a great deal with many people, but if we are to seriously consider such publications we need to be able to look beyond the often unusual formats and try to gauge the intrinsic value of the publication.

Alternative publishing is able to offer a voice to the voiceless, whether directly by encouraging people to make themselves heard, by demystifying the publishing industry and demonstrating that anyone has the potential to communicate their own ideas, or indirectly, by speaking on behalf of those who are unable to make themselves heard. Alternative literature has the capacity to inform, educate and set the record straight on all manner of topics, and frequently does. It also provides endless delight.

In summary we can do no better than quote Michelle Rau writing in *Alternative Press Review* on the forces that drive people towards alternative publishing as: ' [the] rejection of mainstream media, reaction to declining individualism in ... society, the commercialism and profiteering of the mainstream press, the search for community, and the construction of alternative value systems.'[4]

The alternative press has developed unique forms of expression, foremost amongst these being the zine, an independent, small circulation magazine usually edited and written by a single person and done out of pure enthusiasm. In a field where financial constraints prevent many people from producing their own books, the zine offers a relatively cheap means of communicating. The zine is a major element of alternative literature. The subjects covered by zines are immense, ranging from global issues to personal lives; many topics have an outlet only in zines.

From fanzines to zines

Although fanzines (portmanteau for 'fan magazine') began in the days of pulp science fiction, when fans found their books ignored by the mainstream press and determined to create their own fora for discussion, it was the advent of Punk in 1976 that began the self-publishing revolution we see today. Part of the Punk ethic was that it became acceptable, indeed *de rigeur*, to 'learn three chords and form a band'. Bands recorded in bedrooms and cheap, local studios had a few hundred copies of a single pressed and sold it themselves at gigs and through the increasing number of small, independent shops. They bypassed the record companies completely, producing their own records on their own terms.

And as with the sci-fi fans, the followers of this music found expression in fanzines, through titles such as *Sniffin' Glue, Hangin' Around* and *Vague*. Typed or handwritten, photocopied and stapled, sold at gigs and shops, anyone who wanted to could start one. Some lasted for one issue only, the product of enthusiasm over a single record or band, others lasted for years. *Vague* is the only fanzine surviving from the punk explosion of 1977, still sporadic, still mostly the work of its editor, Tom Vague. Its very longevity has garnered esteem from some, accusations of irrelevancy from others. It has recently been awarded some kind of accolade: *The great British mistake: Vague 1977–92* collects a representative selection from its pages, documenting its 'fourteen and a half years' struggle against lies, stupidity and cowardice'. Its historical significance cannot be denied; long interviews with Jon Savage, the Gang of Four, Genesis P. Orridge and Crass, with some remarkably digested writing on the Situationists, the Angry Brigade and post-punk culture.

If anything can provide a touchstone for the myriad sub- and counter-cultural movements in the latter part of the 20th century, the fanzine can. 'Fanzines are the perfect expression – cheaper, more instant than records. Maybe THE medium. A democratisation too – if the most committed "new wave" is about social change then the best fanzines express this. Perhaps most importantly based outside saturated London, they provide a vital function as a base/coordination point of the local scene. And that means Ilford as much as Glasgow. Eventually new inputs, reinterpretation will come from there.'[5]

Now known as zines (pronounced 'zeens'), the ensuing years have seen these publications diversify into all kinds of subjects. They are still most often the product of an individual or small group of friends, acting as writers, designers, publishers and distributors combined. Zine publishing brings together all the characteristics of alternative publishing, but it also establishes communities of interest and enthusiasm outwith the control and commercial necessities not only of mainstream publishing, but of those alternative publishers operating along similar lines. Zine publishing is truly the 'alternative alternative', offering a range of topics, formats, viewpoints and value systems that are unique even within the wider ambit of alternative publishing.

Zines may range in readership from the extremely small (dictated by locale or esoteric interest) to the large and international. They may cover a single, narrow topic obsessively, or range across a number of areas. Some are more like personal journals. Whatever their editor's motives behind publishing – and many are purely for entertainment, which is no bad thing – they are able to guarantee a voice (however fleeting) to anyone who wants to say something. They can bypass even alternative distribution channels, selling direct or exchanging with like-minded publishers in a cashless zine economy. Their erratic, uncontrolled nature and diverse subject matter makes them the print equivalent of the information explosion we have seen more recently on the Internet. Those who have tracked the development of fanzines in the past 20 years will find the protestations of information specialists over the organizational chaos of the Internet wearily familiar. But the zine should not be confused with the lazy, self-indulgent chatter that fills much of the Internet's newsgroups.

Given their diversity and their low circulation; given that they exhibit all the problematic features of alternative literature to an unprecedented degree – why should we trouble to acquire them? What place do they have in libraries? Nobody would propose that we try to acquire these in vast quantities, of course, but even a brief perusal of the subjects they cover will soon discover that there are no other outlets for many of these views; the zines devoted to specific types of music, literature and work are examples of this. They are invariably cheap, and written and designed in styles that will be attractive to a range of readers. They may act as a catalyst for anyone considering publishing themselves – perhaps creative writing groups (which so often find a home in libraries) would find encouragement from such exuberant individual publishing. Although zines are by no means the exclusive province of young people, many would not be out of place in teenage libraries.

Zines are written on all manner of subjects. There are zines about anarchism, all kinds of music, conspiracy theories, dishwashing, sex, comics, board games. All will be different in scope, size, style and content. For those who have never seen a zine, it is impossible to give an accurate flavour of zines in general, but a brief look at a few contrasting titles will give some indication of what they contain and help us to gauge their value.

Some examples of zines

NO LONGER A FANzine is a quintessential zine, produced on a low budget but extremely entertaining and informative. Its primary aim is to communicate with others, to bring people together not for a cause or to buy something or to be entertained as a group, but simply to share their lives with each other. Joseph recounts his travels across the United States, provides anecdotes about the people and the bureaucracy he encounters working in a city information centre, and discusses the various musics and literature in a lengthy series of reviews. Occasional columns and interviews are provided by other zine publishers. Such zines are an important way of sharing ideas, especially for people in small towns and communities who find their interests barely represented or who find themselves marginalized.

Although now defunct, *Wake Up* is a fine example of all that is strong and unique about alternative publishing, combining clear but comprehensive analyses of current affairs with record and gig reviews, mixing interviews with politicians and musicians in equal measure. Remarkably it was the work of one person, Dave T., who wrote, researched, interviewed, typed and distributed the magazine. Defiantly non-profit-making (all profits went to charities and pressure groups) and defiantly exhaustive. The final issue (no.11) of 212 A4 pages, perfect bound, retailed at a mere £3.00. Topics examined in detail included the 'FBI's secret war against the American Indians'; 'the CIA's manipulation of the Labour Party' and a 60-page illustrated essay on the British government's support for state terrorism through arms sales, MI6 and the SAS.

And then there is *The Bug*. There is nothing really like *The Bug*, a double-sided, single colour A4 sheet of epigrams, sayings, observations and the odd drawing. It costs twopence and although described as a 'would-be-monthly' is published whenever 'Ed' feels like it, or when he has enough to fill the pages. Much of it gets close to being poetry; there is a gnomic import to much of the writing that is close to the haiku in execution and effect ('Every book is useless several times a day.' 'We say law when we mean wealth.'). *The Bug* encapsulates much of the ethos of alternative publishing. It's cheap (it couldn't come much cheaper); it's not for profit; it has little to do with self-aggrandisement (it hardly could – how many people have ever heard of it?); it bypasses all the usual channels of distribution (it is only available directly from its editor); it inhabits a culture that is all its own; it defies categorization. And yet it comments on everyday life with a perspicacity and a warmth that is rare.

Baby Sue is written and drawn entirely by one person. Taking its name from the minimalist cartoon character that appears throughout the zine in simple two-panel strips, *Baby Sue* is there primarily to entertain its creator. The humour is by turns cruel, surreal and pointless, yet demonstrates that there is much comic talent to be found outwith the professional cartoonists' anthologies that mostly represent comic art in our bookshops.

Many zines are free for the price of a stamp, an IRC or a stamped, addressed envelope. Collecting a number of these will not only introduce you to some of what zines can offer, they will also open up networking opportunities, one of the best ways of finding your way around alternative literature. *Why...?* is free for the price of an A5 stamped, addressed envelope. Mostly written by its editor Dave (no surname), containing brief articles on whatever interests him – mostly sharp, well-researched articles that get straight to the point on such issues as animal testing, East Timor, nuclear reprocessing, along with guest articles on such diverse topics as rainforest destruction in Canada and the

Vaccination Information Network. *Proletarian Gob* is an anarcho-communist zine, 'anti-capitalist, anti-state and anti-authoritarian', appearing every six months. It includes articles on such topics as 'why we have to abandon the use of the concept and term: democracy', a reprint of part of Raoul Vaneigem's *The revolution of everyday life* and a lively and substantial letters page. *Alphabet Threat* is a tabloid newspaper zine of mostly autobiographical writings that reveals much about the alternative culture. Short, conversational monologues on libertarian education, sexual identity, the pros and cons of infoshops, the value of listening, plus short stories and drawings. Much more than the sum of its parts and of more than local interest. *Underground* sports a sophisticated design rare amongst zines. Its dense black and white overlays, its extreme experimentation with typefaces and sizes and its unsettling graphics all conspire to make parts of it illegible (at times it resembles a monochromatic *Oz*). The articles, by such luminaries as Stewart Home, Sadie Plant and Mark Pawson speak of cyberculture, urban decay, state repression and sexual politics.

Finding out about zines

Information about zines is usually transmitted through zines themselves. Zine publishers are committed networkers, every zine containing at least a listing of that editor's current favourites. There are also a number of review zines. The most comprehensive of these is *Factsheet 5*, calling itself 'the definitive guide to the zine revolution', a bi-monthly of over 100 pages. It relies on the zine publishers' own desires to network and share ideas and their drive for self-publicity. It set out by guaranteeing to review every zine it received, but such is the growth of zine publishing that this is now impossible. But it does not avoid reviewing previously-reviewed titles as new issues appear. The current issue of *Factsheet 5* is therefore always the most accurate snapshot of the whole range of (largely US, Canadian and UK) zines you will find anywhere. The subject headings under which it gathers the titles provide a telling index to the range of zines currently available. These include: work; spirituality; satire; B-movies; science fiction; technology; punk; politics; queer; comix (*sic*); arts and letters; poetry. It also carries selected reviews of books and recordings, and provides updates of other catalogues, directories and networks in all these subjects. *Factsheet 5* is quite simply essential for any exploration of the zine phenomenon.

Until recently *Factsheet 5* was alone, but there is now in Britain a rival, still new, still expanding. This is *Bypass* which, since it focuses on the smaller British scene (although it does include some US and Canadian titles), is still able to review every zine received. It describes itself well as 'simply a tool to enable you to find out what others are doing and communicate, exchange and network on a direct basis, using the magazine for open access to information, entertainment and dissemination'. The stress is not on the product but what can accrue – in informational terms – from networking with the publishers and authors of the titles listed.

Any guide to zines is bound to go out of date extremely quickly. Zines rise and fall so quickly that many are no sooner reviewed than they are unavailable. As former editors of *Factsheet 5*, Mike Gunderloy (its founding editor) and Cari Goldberg Janice know this well. Their book *The world of zines: a guide to the independent magazine revolution* is aimed at the mainstream market and as the years pass has less and less value as a reference work. (Even when first published some of the details were already out of date.) It comprises reprints of reviews from *Factsheet 5*, arranged under the subject headings used by the journal itself. There are some 400 publications listed here, which sounds impressive, but bear in mind that *Factsheet 5* currently features some 1500 zine reviews in each issue. For those who would like a manageable introduction to zines, though, this is a good enough place to start. As an information resource for intending publishers it is especially valuable, for whilst providing an impressive range of examples, there is much practical advice for starting your own zine, looking at production, printing, distribution and finance.

Getting inside the world of zines may not appear easy, but for a regular insider's view of the 'industry' *Obscure* is highly recommended. This is a newszine that offers space for zinesters to debate the current state of zine publishing, to share information about distribution and to advertise their wares. At the time of writing the debate rages over *Factsheet 5*'s decision not to review all the zines it receives – would that such a debate were opened up about *Choice* or the *London Review of Books*!

Michelle Rau's article 'Towards a history of fanzine publishing: from APA to zines'[6] is a very readable introduction to zine publishing and Bob Black's *Beneath the underground* provides an inimitable collection of essays looking closely at zines amongst other areas of alternative publishing. Chris Dodge's bibliography of articles and monographs on zines, *A zine-ography*, provides further alternative (and mainstream) commentaries on the phenomenon. (Dodge also co-edits *MSRRT Newsletter*, an important source of news and reviews of alternative publications – see Chapter 5 for a fuller description.)

Research Publications produce *The Underground and Alternative Press in Britain during [year]*, a microfilm collection of (at present) 24 titles. The rationale behind the choice of titles is unclear, but once chosen they seem to remain in the collection for as long as they continue publishing. Criteria used to replace defunct titles seem equally opaque. The collection at present offers a reasonable enough snapshot of the coverage of alternative periodicals, including gay and lesbian issues (*Rouge*), environmental activism (*Green Anarchist*) and local alternative newspapers. Its inclusion of such newstand stalwarts as *Private Eye* and *Viz* is less convincing. Unfortunately the collection is not indexed. Although it does not cover even one per cent of the periodicals currently published in this country, it could form the basis of a collection.

Copyright and the anti-copyright movement

Copyright is a subject that continues to exercise librarians, and on which millions of words and hours have been spent in entanglement with the law and notions of fair dealing. It is only in the alternative press where you will find the truly radical view of copyright, where there is a strong movement against intellectual property rights and for the full distribution of publications, unhindered by copyright clearance. We might be familiar with this notion in a limited sense from copyright-free educational materials, but some sections of the alternative press take this much further, encouraging unlimited copying.

Because the ethos of much alternative publishing is concerned with the widest possible dissemination of unorthodox, dissident ideas using the smallest amount of resources, many authors and publishers encourage the free circulation of their material. In many books and journals will be found 'anti-copyright' statements (increasingly accompanied by the symbol 'N©'), indicating that the reader or purchaser is free to copy as much of the document as they wish, provided that it is not for commercial purposes. It is expected that those doing so might wish to make a charge to cover their duplicating cost, but this should not include a profit margin. Some titles explicitly encourage the copying and distribution of the work in its entirety, only asking that the original publisher is informed, so that they are kept aware of the number of editions circulating (after all, a small publisher on a tight budget might decide that, due to the number and extent of pirate editions in existence, there is no need for an original reprint. They can, then, channel their energies into new titles). Examples abound: Bob Black's essay, *The Abolition of Work*, besides appearing in the eponymous Autonomedia collection, has been reprinted in dozens of journals and magazines and is currently circulating as a pamphlet in at least two 'pirate' editions. The anti-car tract *Dear motorist ... the social ideology of the motor car* is now only available in such editions, whilst *Radio Sermonettes* by the Moorish Orthodox Radio Collective is largely circulating in Britain as a pirate edition ('May be freely pirated and used – however, please inform us') from the publishers of the review journal *Bypass*. The quality of the reproductions inevitably varies – such editions tend to be photocopies, since the quick and cheap circulation of the ideas is paramount. These might properly be considered the true samizdat publishing of the West.

It would be a mistake to think that all alternative publishers are so keen to have their work thus duplicated. Take care to note the copyright statements in such titles as those from Black Rose Books and South End Press, just as stringent as those of larger publishers. But being aware that such a notion as anti-copyright exists on many titles can have benefits for both the user and for the library. For the user it gives them the freedom to legitimately copy entire documents without any comeback. As a not-for-profit public service it can be argued that a library service could also produce legitimate copies for circulation amongst its branches and departments (though the move towards libraries as commercial enterprises might jeopardize that legitimacy).

Anti-copyright extends well beyond literary reproduction. The *Anti-copyright Catalogue* collects clip-art for dissidents, comprising descriptions of (at the last count) over 200 posters. Any are available for unlimited reproduction for the price of a large, stamped addressed envelope. *Flyposter frenzy: posters from the Anticopyright Network* (edited by Matthew Fuller) brings together just under a hundred of the most-requested posters from the collection in a book, preceded by an informative essay on the history and ideology of the Anti-copyright Network.

Since the advent of musical sampling in the 1980s many musicians and their publishers have taken great pains to establish their rights over the use of even the briefest extract of their music by other musicians. The history of the past ten years is replete with successful prosecutions for unauthorized sampling. From the blatant, large-scale borrowings of Abba by the Justified Ancients of Mu Mu (a.k.a. KLF, a.k.a. Kopyright Liberation Front) to the more subtle – on occasions, undetectable – appropriations of John Oswald and Negativland. Oswald's remixing of Michael Jackson and Negativland's sampling of U2 resulted in near bankruptcy for both, the handing over of master tapes to the plaintiffs and the recall and destruction of all unsold copies of both records. This was especially ironic in Oswald's case, since he had financed and distributed his recording himself – in fact it was never on sale, being circulated free amongst friends and colleagues. The Copyright Violation Squad was founded in 1992 in order to continue to make such recordings available to a wider audience. It argues that however questionable their legal status might be, these works have a cultural value that should not be suppressed. The Negativland case highlights the difference between copyright of the printed word and that of recorded sound. Much of Negativland's work might be considered criticism using the musical medium. Whilst copyright law accepts that brief quotation of the printed word is permissible for the purposes of criticism, musical quotation is considered plagiarism and thus a breach of copyright. At the heart of this debate is the commercial interest which, as we see time after time, is hardly at the heart of alternative publishing.

Whether any library would wish to obtain such materials is a moot point, but the group's occasional *CVS Bulletin* documents the latest news and gives background on these and similar cases. MACOS goes further, aiming to establish a network of musicians who are willing to allow their works to be used for sampling. Such recordings will carry the MACOS logo on their sleeves.

Electronic information: the Internet

The Internet is in a continual state of flux at least as great as that of zine publishing. The two certainly share a common casualness regarding the controls over access. The arrangement and standardization of information approach the extremes of freedom. As with alternative print publishing this can be considered a strength insofar as it encourages democratic access to the technology and use of its data. But the Internet is hardly democratic: the majority of its users are white, middle-class males in academic institutions. This is starting to change with public access terminals in public libraries, and individuals and groups outwith academe placing materials on the system and exchanging ideas and information, but for most people the Internet is still an intangible, more or less meaningless, thing. Let us not, then, look to the Internet as the great leveller, nor as the information saviour. The commercial and governmental forces that instigated it are slowly making themselves felt again and the Internet will not remain as liberatory as it is for much longer. Whether by enforcing specified methods of data transfer and encryption or by introducing widespread charging for services, the resources on the Internet will not endure in their current form. For all that, it remains a remarkable source of alternative information and publications that complement alternative printed sources.

PeaceNet in the US and GreenNet in the UK were founded in 1985 and their linking led to the establishment of the Association for Progressive Communications (APC), which is now the host for other organizations dedicated to social change. They provide not only a cheap method of communicating person to person, but also for electronic conferencing. This can take the form of distributing information (whether in the form of an electronic journal or a database) or for sharing ideas through a debate or forum, between as many people as wish to take part. It is not appropriate to list here all the organizations that are currently part of the APC and to detail their subject interests and the nature of their information. Fortunately Burkhard Luber has already done this in his *The World at Your Keyboard: an alternative guide to global computer networking*. Luber's book not only provides detailed examples of the nature and extent of the information available through the APC on the Internet, but also provides a primer for using the Internet via GreenNet and gives source-by-source examples of how to send mail, take part in conferencing and download information.

Amongst the hundreds of chaotic and mostly useless fan clubs that comprise the newsgroups available via Usenet, there are some useful postings for sources of alternative information in such as misc.activism.progressive, alt.activism and alt.zines. Steve Rimmer's *Planet Internet* calls itself 'an irreverent guide to the Internet's pubs, curiosity shops, and back alleys' and appears to be sold as a guide to alternative resources. In fact it deals mostly with newsgroups, particularly the trivia to be found there. Although a few of the entries featured are useful (Electronic Frontier Foundation, zines), few are treated thoroughly enough for it to provide anything that an afternoon's browse of the newsgroups wouldn't achieve (there is no mention of the key source to zines on the Internet, *Factsheet 5 Electric*, for instance).

There are many activist mailing lists and other e-mail based groups on the Internet, such as ACTIV-L (general activism),

ACT-UP (AIDS Coalition to Unleash Power mailing list), PROG-PUBS (progressive campus publications), SAPPHO (lesbian and bisexual women) and SEACnet (Student Environmental Action Coalition). (Details of all these have been posted on the misc.activism.progressive newsgroup.) There is a gopher site (gopher: iia.org) in New Jersey run by the Digital Freedom Network that is making banned texts available through the Internet. Gary Sick of Human Rights Watch in New York is setting up a gopher site to bring together the work of such human rights groups as his own, Amnesty International, PEN and *Index on Censorship*.

The World Wide Web

The advent of the World Wide Web (WWW) has not only widened access to information on the Internet, it has also improved the presentation and downloading of information. Browsers like WebCrawler make it easier to navigate through the ever-increasing networks. Through WWW we will find EnviroWeb, the clearing-house for all online environmental information, both mainstream and alternative. The NativeNet World-Wide Web Site allows access to a wide variety of information resources (including journals and bibliographies) related to indigenous peoples around the world on other WWW sites, gopher sites, mailing lists and newsgroups. There is the Internet Directory of Published Writers, an unmediated directory to which anyone may append their own entry. *Factsheet 5*'s electronic version, *Factsheet 5 Electric*, is available via the San Francisco Whole Earth 'Lectronic Link (The WELL) and from Stanford University.

Spunk Press is an especially impressive electronic archive of anarchist and situtationist literature spread across a number of sites in Europe and the US. It includes classic anarchist texts by Bakunin and Goldman alongside contemporary analyses by Chomsky and Castoriadis, as well as the full text of many anarchist journals, bibliographies, reading lists and an array of pointers to other related WWW sites.

The popularity of the Internet has resulted in a number of alternative cyberspace magazines such as *bOING bOING* (sic) and *Wired* going overground and becoming internationally distributed through mainstream channels. There do remain a number of magazines within alternative publishing, however, although whether they too will seek wider audiences remains to be seen. *3W* examines Internet access from the point of view of the people that make up the virtual communities of the Internet, rather than as a business opportunity or a time-wasting leisure activity. It provides much useful information – aimed at beginners and the more adept – on the techniques of access, as well as providing overviews (and addresses) for electronic zines, Gopher and WWW Jewels, newsgroups and bulletin boards. *The Message* looks at alternative online services such as Fidonet and dial-up bulletin boards as well as the Internet and publicizes the work of CommUnity, a pressure group that represents the interests of the independent UK online community against the interests of corporate business and government.

References

1. Maurice Line, 'Knowledge is power, and power is dangerous', *Library Association Record* **92**(11) November 1990, pp. 829–32, 835.
2. Charles Willett, 'Politically controversial monographs: roles of publishers, distributors, booksellers, *Choice* magazine, and librarians in acquiring them for academic libraries', *Building on the first century: proceedings of the Fifth National Conference of the Association of College and Research Libraries*, Cincinnati, Ohio, April 5–8, 1989, Association of College and Research Libraries, 1989, pp. 238–41.
3. John Quail, *The slow burning fuse* (London: Paladin, 1978), p. xiv.
4. Michelle Rau, 'Towards a history of fanzine publishing: from APA to zines', *Alternative Press Review*, Spring/Summer 1994, pp.10–13.

5. Jon Savage, *England's Dreaming: Sex Pistols and Punk Rock* (London: Faber and Faber, 1991), p. 401.

6.   Michelle Rau, op. cit.

2 The Subjects of Alternative Literature – a General Guide

Put simply, we can consider alternative literature as providing information and knowledge across the same broad categories that are typically considered as constituents of a library's mainstream collection. In other words, we shall find publications dealing with the informational and the educational; the social and the political; the cultural and the recreational. But as we have already seen, the themes within each of these categories will extend our information and knowledge, since they provide new and unknown perspectives on subjects we already recognize, at the same time as they offer us entirely new subjects for investigation. To understand this in action let us examine the dominant topics in alternative literature, beginning with an area that might be considered as the foundation of all the others.

Critiques of public life and the mass media

One of the main imperatives of the alternative press is to set the record straight, to offer critiques of the organizations that dominate public life, whether governments or businesses. Given the close links between government and business, such critiques are of especial value to understanding the controls under which we all live. They are of value as they help us to fathom the economic and political imperatives by which we are governed, and how other people in other countries are governed.

From the viewpoint of most writers in the alternative press, the mass media are complicit in this, being an integral part of the business-government nexus. Consequently critiques of the dominant methods of reporting are equally essential to these studies. Driven more by justice than by commerce, alternative literature is often the home for investigative journalism; investigations undertaken in areas where the mainstream cannot (due to reporting restrictions), or will not (due to commercial pressures).

This is such a crucial role of the alternative press, which underpins the entire alternative publishing enterprise, that it will be examined in detail in the next chapter.

Environmental activism

'Environmentally responsible', 'green' products are now commonplace on our supermarket shelves. The greening of business and the coverage of environmental issues such as pollution from motorized transport, chemical dumping, acid rain and CFC production seems to indicate that such concerns have finally been adopted by the mainstream. All major publishers now carry a number of environmental titles; all bookshops now have a section devoted to it. What more can possibly need saying about this topic? But in common with many other radical and alternative ideas, the adoption of environmentalism by the mainstream has been very much on the mainstream's terms. In terms of a social revolution, this adoption of the environmental agenda has had little effect. Although it is largely recognized that the only thoroughgoing solution to environmental disasters that are the result of large-scale corporate and urban profligacy is a return to local community empowerment and human-scale institutions, we are just as far from these as we were when Leopold Kohr first published his ideas in *The Breakdown of Nations* or when they were popularized in the 1960s in Schumacher's *Small is Beautiful*.

As once-radical philosophies such as recycling, waste reduction and green transport become mainstream, so other, more radical ideas fill up the space they leave, and environmental activists attempt change through other means. Just as what is now commonplace was obscure and hard to come by a decade ago, the cutting-edge of today's environmental activism is still firmly in the province of the alternative media. *Earth First! Journal* documents that organization's many international direct protest actions (they have been much in evidence in the protests against wilderness destruction in the US and against the UK government's road-building programme) and provides the worldwide network of Earth First! groups with information on successful (and not so successful) tactics. But it goes further than merely documenting campaigns: it provides detailed ecological information on all the current campaign sites, alongside equally informed histories of the practices of the businesses and governments involved. Each issue also contains listings for all the known Earth First! groups worldwide, as well as book reviews and information on other groups sympathetic to Earth First!'s aims. By contrast, *Wild Earth* is more academically slanted, less committed to direct action (this is interesting since its founder, Dave Foreman, also helped to found Earth First!). It may be considered as a counterpoint to *Earth First! Journal* and certainly inhabits more common ground with it than with *Society and Nature*, a hefty 200-page scholarly journal subtitled 'The international journal of political ecology', featuring such writers as Murray Bookchin, Noam Chomsky and Cornelius Castoriadis.

Green Anarchist, like *Earth First! Journal*, is a tabloid newspaper that also looks beyond its own country. It too acts as a campaigners' focus, this time for activities in the UK, but it also reports from all over the world. Its masthead slogan, 'For a free society in harmony with nature', indicates its spread of interests and examines notions of freedom in society as well as environmental activism. It carries regular critiques of the liberal mainstream campaigning groups such as Greenpeace and British Union for the Abolition of Vivisection and provides invaluable unmediated information about the more militant groups such as the Animal Liberation Front. Its extensive review section includes items from the alternative and the mainstream press, frequently critical of both. *Greenline* has for over a decade been a networking tool for environmental activists in Britain, documenting actions, demonstrations and conferences and providing a detailed diary of forthcoming events. Still resolutely the product of the activists themselves, there is little room here for theoretical analysis; the writing is descriptive and informative on extremely current issues. *Planetary Connections* and *Planet News* (a free newspaper) perform similar, if less comprehensive, functions.

Central to environmental activism is the planning and establishment of 'intentional communities' that put into practice permaculture, the cashless economy (through LETS – Local Economy Trading Schemes, discussed by Peter Lang in his *LETS work: rebuilding the local economy*) and the application of alternative technologies. *TRANET* digests news and articles from almost a thousand periodicals that deal with such movements and communities. In the UK, *Fourth World Review* ('For small nations, small communities and the human spirit') promotes human-scale communities and economics, and regularly examines publications that share its aims. Details of the communities themselves will be found in (for the UK) *Diggers and Dreamers: the guide to communal living* and (for the US) *Directory of Intentional Communities: a guide to co-operative living*. *dreamtime talkingmail* (sic) is the magazine of Dreamtime Village, an intentional community in Wisconsin that is attempting to combine traditional methods of permaculture with 'the hypermedia arts'. It regularly includes reviews of underground publications. *Clean Slate*, the journal of the Alternative Technology Association of the UK, is a slim quarterly that began as a reporting medium for developments in alternative technology. It has since expanded its brief to cover sustainable development in other forms and now features other topics such as organic gardening and permaculture. It contains mostly short articles, but it is still valuable for a popular update on the alternative energy scene in the UK. The Intermediate Technology Development Group publish an extensive catalogue of books and reports that look at sustainable and appropriate technology from all over the world.

Peace and antimilitarism

The role of local and national activist groups in producing and distributing literature should not be underestimated. It is most noticeable in the fields of peace work and human rights. We have already noted the work of such groups as TAPOL and the Campaign Against Arms Trade when discussing the mass media. The primary research in this and similar areas is mostly done by NGOs, and it is through the activities of their members that such topics are brought to a wider public, becoming matters for debate in government and the mainstream media. Unless we want to wait years for the mainstream media to cover such topics, it is to the alternative press we should look for the place of NGOs in the provision of alternative information.

Campaign Against Arms Trade (CAAT) produces a bi-monthly newsletter that, although intended as a campaigning tool, provides information on other organizations with related aims, as well as first-hand reports and news digests relating to arms sales and purchases throughout the world. Each issue alerts readers to recent publications in its field, both in the mainstream (*UK Defence Statistics*) and from alternative publishers and other NGOs (*Stockholm International Peace Research Institute Yearbook*). CAAT also produces a 'Campaign materials and publications' list which includes books, pamphlets, briefings and videos on the arms trade.

There are many special interest diaries that have more than a trivial value as sources of reference. The prime example is *Housman's Peace Diary and World Peace Directory*. The directory occupies roughly one-third of the diary and is a comprehensive listing of some 2000 peace groups and their publications throughout the world. It emphasizes grassroots organizations including the smaller, local activist organizations as well as the national and international networks. It also includes the more well-known environmental and human rights groups where these are of use to peace campaigners. An appendix provides a regional directory for Britain. The entire directory is also available on GreenNet, where it is supplemented by directories for the rest of the world.

The brief guide *War and peace in the Balkans: a resource guide to ex-Yugoslavia* contains information on peace groups in the former Yugoslavia and those supporting them in the US, along with lists of core printed, video and computer resources. Importantly, it also contains a list of the independent media working in the region, since – in its own words – 'little or no press coverage is given to the work of the anti-war groups and individuals in the region ... Little space is provided for reports from Balkan journalists who work independently from the government-controlled media and provide non-nationalistic perspectives on events.'

Peace News is a monthly tabloid newspaper published cooperatively with War Resisters International (WRI) and incorporating the former *WRI Newsletter*. Consequently much of the paper is given over to news about conscientious objectors throughout the world, along with campaigns to promote and work against militarism. We should note again the networking value of such a publication: names and addresses of individuals and organizations are appended to most of the articles and news items (current issues can help update and amend the entries in *Housman's Peace Diary and World Peace Directory*). *Peace News* also covers conflicts around the world from an antimilitaristic point of view: a remarkable and unique achievement.

Human rights

Human rights organizations and periodicals directory, published by the Meiklejohn Civil Liberties Institute, interprets human rights very widely, and includes details of groups and periodicals dealing with civil liberties, children's and women's rights and environmental and peace issues, making it a valuable resource for many of the topics discussed in the present chapter. Amnesty International is perhaps the best known of human rights organizations, though its reports and periodicals (the bi-monthly

Amnesty and its monthly *International Newsletter*) are rarely found in libraries outwith academia, despite their non-academic style and non-specialist concerns. In fact, much human rights information (and the publications of NGOs generally) is equally rare in our public libraries. Human Rights Watch is the major independent organization monitoring and publicizing human rights violations throughout the world in its extensive series of books and reports. The Minority Rights Group is an NGO working 'to secure justice for minority groups who are suffering discrimination, and for the peaceful co-existence of majority and minority communities'. It publishes a series of brief reports and in-depth monographs, along with the *World Directory of Minorities*. At the commercial end of alternative publishing, but still providing much information on human rights resources in an approachable, popular style, is the glossy, large circulation monthly *New Internationalist*. The Data Center's *Third World Resources* is a quarterly review of resources from and about the Third World, including lists of organizations, books, periodicals and other publications. The Data Center also publishes a series of directories, each focusing on a geographical area (Africa, Middle East) or topic (human rights, peace and justice), each containing extensive resource lists.

Freedom of speech and censorship

There is not an alternative publication or publisher that is not touched by issues of freedom of speech or censorship. Whether it is Mike Diana's prosecution for his allegedly obscene comic book *Boiled Angel* (he has been forbidden to draw anything 'obscene' – his probation officer may enter his house without a warrant to check on him) or the UK security services' harassment of *Green Anarchist*, the history of alternative publishing is packed with examples of draconian measures taken against small circulation, non-commercial titles. This is all the more ironic when much alternative publishing sets out explicitly to discover and expose the secretive workings of government, business and the mass media. It also challenges the boundaries of what is permissible, and works to increase and to normalize the twin freedoms of information and expression. Such efforts are an integral part of alternative publishing and many of the titles described in this book (particularly in the areas of media criticism and sexual politics) document such challenges.

Margaret Thatcher's former press secretary Bernard Ingham declared in 1986 that 'there is no freedom of information in this country [the UK] ... Bugger the people's right to know. The game is in the security of the state – not the public's right to know.[1] This avowed premium on information has led to the rise of many campaigning groups working to obtain greater public access to governmental and commercial information.

The Campaign for Freedom of Information publishes a quarterly newspaper *Secrets*, containing updates on all British examples of secrecy in local and national government, along with the parliamentary efforts to counter such secrecy. It also produces an extensive range of publications: books, reports and lecture transcripts detailing what legislation needs to be put in place to combat official secrecy, restrictions on access to environmental information, corporate safety and medicines. In the US, newsletters such as the National Campaign for Freedom of Expression's *NCFE Bulletin* and the American Civil Liberties Union's *Arts Censorship Project Newsletter* perform similar functions.

Index on Censorship, after years as an A4 magazine, is now publishing bimonthly as a perfect bound journal of some 250 pages. Its essential features remain: eyewitness reporting from around the world on all aspects of free speech and its repression and the 'Index Index', a chronicle of state censorship arranged by country, updated in every issue. (It is particularly disturbing how the entries for Britain and the US have now expanded, rivalling the classic examples of states such as China and South Africa.) In its expanded form the journal can now range widely with lengthy essays from all manner of political and social commentaries from the broad left. This is the only journal looking at censorship in such detail and with such authority, digesting research by groups such as Article 19, Human Rights Watch, International PEN and drawing on a battery of specialist commentators, reporters and writers.

The *Directory of Libertarian Periodicals*, although a cheap, typed and photocopied list, is a compact guide to journals and organizations promoting laissez-faire individualism, free from governmental interference. In the UK, the Libertarian Alliance is an especially prolific publisher, with a catalogue of hundreds of reports, pamphlets, notes and study guides covering all manner of legal and commercial, public and private issues from a libertarian stance.

Anarchism

Anarchy might be considered as a paradigm of alternative publishing – not in its populist equation with chaos, but as social relationships based on voluntary cooperation. Notions of individual freedom, unfettered by commercial or governmental interference; enterprises run on collective lines; the importance of diversity of opinion in publications; these are all anarchist ideals. For many alternative publishers they can be realized by writing and publishing themselves. Donald Rooum has declared that 'Anarchists believe that the point of society is to widen the choices of individuals'[2] and that all anarchist thought and action proceeds from that. In essence, anarchism is concerned with challenging authority, questioning its legitimacy and helping people take control of their own lives and, consequently, of the societies in which they live. Insofar as it challenges authority, anarchism is against the state and for direct, fully participative democracy.

Anarchists are responsible for an immense number of titles in alternative publishing, from the long-standing anarchist fortnightly newspaper *Freedom* and its sister quarterly *The Raven* to the newer, but more detailed and exhaustive contents of journals such as *Fifth Estate*, *Anarchy* and *Black Flag*.

Although it is not possible for it to be as current as the fortnightly *Freedom*, the coverage in *Fifth Estate* is much more detailed, offering analyses and op-ed columns, in addition to retrospective pieces on major anarchist figures such as Emma Goldman. It has a large book review section and pages of readers' letters. Some of the most serious, well-informed and inspiring anarchist writing is to be found here. The intellectual meat of the 80 or so pages that make up each quarterly issue of *Anarchy: a journal of desire armed* is the theoretical articles on anarchy, but its practical value as a networking and selection tool lies in its extensive 'alternative media review' section, its reports of international anarchist news and the pages and pages of readers' letters (in some issues these can fill half the journal). *Black Flag* provides a comprehensive national and international anarchist news service, networking information about current protests and updates about information centres throughout Britain. Unsigned articles will be found next to articles by Noam Chomsky. The journal cuts through much of the obscurantism and pretention that bedevils much radical political writing, proof that radical ideas can be expressed simply and clearly, without any hint of patronization.

Bob Erler's *Anarchist Booklist* is an inexpensive and compact guide to what for many is a sprawling, almost unmanageable area of alternative publishing. Erler presents compilations of, amongst others, introductory books on anarchism; collections of literature; anarchist classics; theory; history; biography and 'hagiography'. It is a manageable selection, brief, and helpfully annotated. *Anarchist Year Book* is another cheap directory of resources. Currently running at 32 pages, it provides three listings, 'not meant as authoritative but exploratory'. The first contains anarchist publishers and organizations in Britain, from the long established Freedom Press to the self-published titles of Derrick A. Pike. The second listing is of British periodicals. The yearbook begins with a useful list of all anarchist titles published in Britain in the preceding year. Each book, periodical and organization is briefly described.

The titles of London's Freedom Press feature prominently in Erler's list and as the world's foremost anarchist publisher and distributor for over 100 years this should come as no surprise. Their own publications are conspicuous by their use of clear and simple language, their concision and their low price. Three useful places to start are: Donald Rooum's *What is Anarchism?* – a simple introduction featuring representative extracts from all the major writers on anarchism, including Bakunin, Kropotkin, Malatesta, William Morris; John Griffin's examination of the practical nature of anarchy, *A Structured Anarchism*, and Colin Ward's look at strategies in *Anarchy in Action*. The major UK distributors for anarchist publications are AK Press and Distribution and A Distribution. In addition to their catalogues, the *New Anarchist Review* provides quarterly updates and brief reviews of new titles. In the US, Perennial Books supplies both mainstream and alternative anarchist publications. Its catalogue runs from the classic works of theory to the modern tracts and pamphlets. Entries are interspersed with original essays and extracts from the texts themselves, putting much of the catalogue instantly and easily into context.

Situationist literature

There are close links between anarchism and the situationist movement, despite the relatively short time that situationist ideas have been in currency. The seminal works were published by the Situationist International (SI) in 1967: Guy Debord's *The society of the spectacle* and Raoul Vaneigem's *The revolution of everyday life*. In essence, situationists identified that life was increasingly being lived not by direct experience but by simulacra, by representations of that life. The individual was no longer taking any active part in society, simply observing it passively, as one does a circus, a television programme or some other spectacle. The 'mission' of the SI and its adherents was to alert people to the nature of this 'spectacular society' and to encourage individual and collective action against it. The situationists proposed constructing situations, including what Debord called 'momentary ambiences of life', leading to the full-blown redesigning of cities ('unitary urbanism') in order to revitalize people in their communities and environments. Much of current media studies have at their centre the simple premise of the situationists. The technique of *détournement*, the appropriation of cultural artefacts and their reworking to 'reveal' their hidden power, has given birth to the 'culture jamming' and 'subvertising' (which we will encounter in the next chapter) and influenced the punk graphics of Jamie Reid and a thousand imitators. John Yates is one of the more original artists employing this technique. His major work comprises taking photographs in the public domain from advertisements, school books, newspapers etc. and adding captions to them that distort or redefine (*détourne*) their meaning.

The *Spectacular Times* series was begun by the late Larry Law in the 1980s. These little (A6) booklets, out of print for a few years, are slowly being reprinted by A Distribution. Each offers a situationist critique of one aspect of modern life, using simple text counterpointed by detourned graphic, photographs and quotations from the mass media. Subjects include the mass media themselves, women and animal rights.

Simon Ford's bibliography of situationist literature and Bob Black's little bibliography in *Beneath the underground*[3] are places to start for an exhaustive examination of the plethora of statements, gestures and artworks that have been inspired by Debord, Vaneigem and the SI. A selection of situationist literature will be found in the catalogues of A Distribution, AK Distribution, Counter Productions and most other catalogues that include anarchist and related literature.

Critical education and free schools

Although we will find political parties that promote the parents' freedom to choose their children's education, none will go so far as to actively encourage forms of education that challenge the notion of schooling so radically as do the advocates of free schools. Libertarian education, of which free schools are but one manifestation, aims to return the power of learning to the child or the student, encouraging parents and other adults to help develop the child's learning, rather than impose a structure on the child. Organizations such as Human Scale Education and Play For Life both publish their own periodical, along with a range of booklets and other materials to support such initiatives.

In Britain there has been much government and business promotion of 'transferable skills', seen as essential in an 'education for life'. Information and knowledge skills are amongst these and there has been increasing government intervention in curriculum development throughout schools, colleges and universities to ensure that such skills are taught. The response of many teachers has been to look closely at enabling students to think for themselves and to examine methods that not only teach them how to find information but to introduce them to all possible forms of information and help them make informed choices amongst what they read. One of the major works about encouraging such critical and independent learning is published by an alternative publisher, Black Rose Books of Montreal. This is *Critical teaching and everyday life* by Ira Shor who, in applying the work of the pedagogue Paolo Freire to university open admissions students, laid the groundwork for critical thinking and critical teaching practices in higher education. Black Rose also publish Joel Spring's pocket-sized *Primer of libertarian education*, a very readable history of radical education in Britain and the US and *Between the lines: how to detect bias and propaganda in the media and everyday life* by Eleanor MacLean. This material is radical enough to warrant distribution through alternative channels, yet its harmonization with the developing orthodoxy of student-centred learning might lead one to think that such ideas might be assimilated by mainstream educational publishers.

Yet we still seem as far from the general acceptance of libertarian educational methods as we were when A.S. Neill founded Summerhill between the two world wars. It is still amongst the small presses that we must look for both the historical documentation and current developments in this field. Libertarian Education is a publishing collective which for over 25 years has promoted alternatives to mainstream schooling within and without the state and private systems in Britain. It also maintains a role as a focus for the promotion of educational initiatives from all over the world. Its termly journal *LibED* acts as a practical guide to curriculum development and ideas for use in classroom teaching and home education. Its autumn and summer issues are A4 magazines, the spring issue a perfect bound journal on a single theme (1994's was 'play') and features articles by teachers, educationalists and students. Libertarian Education's key mono-graph is *Freedom in education: a do-it-yourself guide to the liberation of learning*. Beginning with a simple introduction in the style of the Freedom Press books mentioned earlier, the main body of the book divides into two: curriculum articles and resources. The curriculum articles provide discussion and ideas for teaching; the resources listed include a bibliography of books on libertar-ian education, a directory of groups supportive of these initia-tives and who can provide resources for teaching and an international list of organizations promoting freedom in educa-tion. (There is also a subject index to the first 50 issues of *LibED*.)

The book also provides an introduction to the work of Education Otherwise, set up in 1977 to provide advice and sup-port to children and parents who want an education at home, or otherwise outwith the control of the established school system. Its own publications list contains introductions to the work of Montessori, Steiner and Holt, and offers practical guides to learning at home for all ages from early years to teenagers. The group also publishes a bi-monthly newsletter, as does its parallel organization in the USA, Growing without Schooling, which also produces the *Homeschooling Resource List*. John Holt, the founder of Growing without Schooling, is the author of a num-ber of books on libertarian education in the US, including *Teach your own*, *Learning all the time* and *How children learn, how children fail*. These and similar titles form a useful selected bibliography in Love and Rage Community Society's *A Deschooling reader: alternatives, analysis and ideas for doing things better*, which might be considered the Canadian equivalent of *Freedom in education*. Grace Llewellyn's *The teenage liberation handbook: how to quit school and get a real life and education* is aimed directly at students themselves in their teenage years and aims to give them confi-dence to 'drop out' and develop their own educational pro-grammes with their families and local communities, now that home schooling is legal in most US states. Llewellyn also pro-duces a quarterly zine, *Unschooling Ourselves*.

Work, zerowork and play

Most protests against work that are reported in the mainstream media are simply against working conditions, and are mediated through the large trade unions, which themselves now operate as businesses. Direct participation in union activity is now very difficult. Unions are specialized, with little solidarity between sectors during strikes. Anti-union legislation and the anti-union actions of many transnational companies are forcing many large unions to abandon direct action in favour of boardroom discussion. But there are organizations and publications that promote direct worker participation in improving their lot and encourage workers from all sectors to work together.

Journals such as *Libertarian Labor Review* and *Industrial Worker*, the journal of the small international, inter-sector union the Industrial Workers of the World (IWW) report internationally on workers' attempts to organize within the workplace, across employment sectors and across countries. Both are anti-state and for self-management: concepts that do not feature in any mainstream union's aims. Whilst both are useful for gaining more information about these and similar movements, *Libertarian Labor Review* features extensive book reviews and regular contact lists for other publications and organizations relevant to radical unionism. *Burning Fuse* is compiled by the British end of the IWW. All these journals provide critiques of both management practices and divisive union structures, and provide union and worker news, local and international.

At the more specialized end of the scale we will find journals and zines aimed precisely at a single job specialism. The best source for an overview of what is available is in the 'Work' section of *Factsheet 5*, where we will find publications for socially responsible electrical engineers (*Short circuit*), airline employees (*The Steward*), neon sign crafters (*Neon News*) and even dishwashers (*Dishwasher*).

There are some who question the whole notion of work. Such authors find themselves even further outside the mainstream: despite the much-vaunted advent of the leisure age, we are all still working just as much as we ever did. The only ones saved from this are the unemployed, but they have their own problems. The futurologists of the early 1970s promised mass unemployment but saw automation as our deliverance from drudgery. This has not happened and no political party will countenance a world without work. Bob Black is the foremost commentator here, coining the term 'zerowork' for his thesis that 'work is the source of nearly all the misery in the world'. His landmark essay, 'The abolition of work', first appeared in *The abolition of work and other essays* and continues to be reprinted in pamphlets and journals all over the world. Black is co-editor of *Zerowork: the anti-work anthology* with Tad Kepley and an especially acerbic commentator on alternative publishing itself, being one of its few significant essayists. A zine like *The Idler* (describing itself as 'literature for loafers') looks at the lives of those without work but who manage to enjoy it, provides inspiration for those wanting to move towards this particular Nirvana.

With the abolition of work will come the rise of play. Much alternative publishing not only has play as its theme; play is also its main function. We have already encountered zines written purely for entertainment. There are some presses that devote themselves wholly to playful activity, that are clearly extensions of their creators' desire to enjoy themselves, free from any sobre connotations that the publishing industry might have. Playtime For Ever Press is the supreme example of this, producing a range of broadsheets, magazines, tiny booklets and uncategorizable items all dedicated to the pursuit of play, or promoting play as the apogee of human endeavour. Their tiny (A7, 4pp) booklets reproduce their earlier *Penny Dreadful* sheets: 400 word texts within delicate, marbled covers, offering titles such as *Demolish serious buildings* and *Play is everything work is not*. They are dedicated to re-introducing joy and pleasure into daily life, affirmed by their enthused language and inspired packaging. The press's own zine *Fatuous Times* collects many of these pieces, whilst its Zine Tester – a small phial of colourless liquid – attempts to solve all the problems of zine acquisition. A single drop on a zine under consideration will indicate 'how excellent' the zine is: 'if it turns a bright orange you've got a winner!'

Sexual politics

This is another topic that, in common with environmental activism, has been taken up by the mainstream to a great degree. But as with environmental activism, as aspects of it have been made available through the mainstream (AIDS education, gay and lesbian fiction, gay and lesbian politics), so the gap in the alternative literature has been filled by literature that to date has been resistant to incorporation into the mainstream – gay and lesbian zines, militant gay activism, the proclamation of 'other' sexualities on equal terms to the dominant 'heteroculture'. Turnaround Distribution has a separate catalogue for gay and lesbian titles, featuring over 60 publishers, mostly independents such as Millivres Books and St. Martin's Press. Publications such as *The Lesbian Review of Books* cover an even wider range, whether for acquisition or research. The Women's Studies Librarian at the University of Wisconsin publishes a range of titles that feature alternative publications prominently, such as *Feminist collections: a quarterly of women's studies resources* and *Feminist periodicals: a current listing of contents.*

There is no shortage of newspapers and magazines written by and for gays and lesbians. Many of these have now become familiar on our newsstands (*Gay Scotland, Gay Times, The Pink Paper*) but we should not ignore the numerous local and national zines that have sprung up. Whilst many of these are reviewed in *Factsheet 5* (*Magazines for Libraries* also contains a valuable section on gay and lesbian periodicals), the specialist source is *Queer Zine Explosion*, which reviews almost a hundred gay and lesbian titles in every issue, along with a little music and a few books. (Its editor, Larry-Bob, also edits his own well-respected zine, *Holy Titclamps.*) For the UK, *Qz* performs a similar function and provides a listing of British zines 'with a queer/feminist slant'.

Alternative literature is also home to many 'sex-positive' publications, where sexual preferences considered as perversities by many mainstream commentators (or as 'too hot to handle' by mainstream publishers and distributors) are able to be expressed. This might be considered another facet of the freedom of expression that alternative publishing encourages. Here we will find publications dealing with sado-masochism, cross-dressing, fetishism, transsexuals. These range from unabashed erotic (pornographic?) literature to how-to manuals and volumes on sex health. There is no doubt that without such publications and their attendant networks many people would have continued to feel that their sexuality – and their lives as a whole – were somehow lesser than those that are represented by the mainstream media. Alternative sexual literature can also have a positive educational and socializing impact, increasing the profile of many marginalized sexual activities, even redefining our notions of obscenity and pornography. Many of these are carried by the generalist distributors such as AK and Left Bank. Richard Kadrey's two *Covert Culture* sourcebooks and the Amok catalogue also feature such titles. The most comprehensive review source is the US tabloid magazine *EIDOS* (*Everyone Is Doing Outrageous Sex*). This is a rare magazine indeed, one that deals with all sexual practices maturely, as the healthy activities of consenting adults, and provides erotic literature, essays on sexual health and freedom of expression and book and product reviews in equal measure. It is not unusual for *EIDOS* to review hundreds of books, journals, zines and newsletters in a single issue, making it the most comprehensive specialist review journal this author has found. For those unable to obtain *EIDOS*, *Factsheet 5* is the best place to begin.[4] Chris Dodge's *Alternative sex: some 'zines, comics, books, and sources* provides a brief, manageable introduction to the field.[5]

Paranormal and Fortean phenomena

There is no shortage of mainstream publications dealing with stories of UFO abductions, ghosts, telekinesis and other inexplicable events. Most of these are little more than unreflective coffee table books, published more for their sensationalism and entertainment value, rather than for any serious value as research projects. And despite the academic kudos that has accrued to this field of study (which has seen the establishment of a chair of parapsychology at the University of Edinburgh), most of the academic material is turgid and far from popular in style. The alternative press is where we will find a much wider spread of opinions, theories and documentation. For many years the primary British journal documenting and commenting upon Fortean phenomena was the staunchly neutral *Fortean Times*. This was also a major source of reviews and information about other publications, organizations and projects. Its subsequent transformation into a newsstand stalwart has seen a reduction in its informational content, and its reviews and networking service is now minimal (this has been noted of many alternative journals that have become mainstream). Its content is now geared more to the sensationalist, although much of interest is still to be found there. But there are other journals that remain unreconstructed alternatives. *Magonia* and *Promises and Disappointments* are edited by long-time researchers who take a critical, rationalist approach to these fields ('interpreting contemporary vision and belief', *Magonia*'s subtitle, sums up their approach). Both typically review and provide addresses and subscription information for dozens of other journals, organizations, books and pamphlets. Moving further out into the areas of occult philosophy, alchemy, Hermeticism, witchcraft, demonology, Chthonios Books is a valuable source of small and fine press publications, many of them available only in extremely limited editions. A key journal for Hermetic studies is *Caduceus*.

The darker side of social change: the literature of the extreme right

If the publications described in this book share one characteristic it is that their alternative views of the world are based on equality, social justice and the responsible use of power. Their existence promotes freedom of expression; their contents advocate and advance freedom of information. The diversity of opinions in the examples provided should be evidence enough of that. Yet freedom of expression is a double-edged sword: as Noam Chomsky has said: 'if you believe in freedom of speech, you believe in freedom of speech for views you don't like.'[6] In other words, if we are setting out to promote alternative publications, should we not also consider titles that represent views that we don't like? Many librarians might not be in sympathy with the views expressed in the titles so far described in this book, just as there is no need for them to be in sympathy with any of the material they acquire. Notwithstanding legal constraints, should librarians not consider material of any nature? Since the information exists, librarians should be expected to find it and acquire it.

Of the distributors mentioned in this book only two, Amok and Loompanics Unlimited, stock material that might be considered as publications from the far right. The ethos of the 'Parallax' section of Amok's catalogue is hard to fathom: it contains items on state terrorism, alongside the writings of Marcus Garvey and volumes dealing with the history of occult conspiracy theories and secret societies. But it also contains items founded on notions of racial supremacy and racial pride, in particular the works of white supremacists and Nazism, along with its avatars and heirs. Amongst the directories listed in Chapter 5, only *From far left to extreme right* mentions periodicals of the far right. The main distribution channels for this literature are quite different from those discussed in this book. Given their controversial nature it is inevitable that much of it goes underground, being privately published and distributed. Despite the authors' and publishers' desires to further their causes, this material tends to be circulated amongst a narrow audience not for reasons of economy, rather for reasons of security and legality. Neither will we find their periodicals indexed in either mainstream or alternative indexes and abstracts (there is no *The Right Index* to balance *The Left Index*).

There is reason to be wary of advising the librarian or researcher to contact known groups such as the British National Party, given their well-reported record of violence against ethnic groups and any they deem to be on the side of ethnic groups: Freedom Books in London and AK Press in Edinburgh are but two organizations which have been regular victims of far right intimidation and violence. If you feel that you must obtain material direct from such sources, then talk to a researcher or a librarian who already has some expertise in this field. The author's experiences with dozens of radical groups including those listed in this book (and even including direct action groups such as Earth First! and the Animal Liberation Front) have all been profitable and easy-going; experiences with far right groups much less so. There are a few sources that, by virtue of their 'academic respectability', are safer to deal with. *Revisionist Researcher* and the Institute for Historical Review are two such, providing scholarly research adducing evidence in support of Holocaust Revisionism.

The arts: fiction and poetry

Just as play has a crucial function in learning (and as an antidote to work) and should not be ignored, neither should we ignore the encyclopaedic range of artistic activity that is created through and commented upon by alternative literature. To fully know the cultural life of any country, region or town one needs to be aware of the myriad styles of music, fiction, poetry and illustration that only exist within alternative literature. To which we can add art forms such as mail art and rubber stamp art, whose only manifestation is through these channels. The arts of the mainstream barely scratch in the surface of this diversity and profusion. The number of fiction titles alone (leaving aside poetry, which if anything is even more ubiquitous) is probably enough to swamp the total of mainstream novels published each year. Experimental literature (what Atlas calls 'enthused writing') much of it surrealist, is the stock-in-trade of such established small publishers as Atlas Press, Dalkey Archive, Exact Change and Serpent's Tail.

The bulk of literary publishing, though, will be found in the chapbooks, journals and zines published by the dozens of small publishers throughout the world. There are far too many to even sample representatively. Journals such as *Bogg: an Anglo-American journal* and *New Hope International*, both stalwarts of the small press literary scene for over 20 years, publish their own substantial review journals (*Bogg Reviews* and *New Hope*

International Review) of new poetry and prose in English from around the world. Dustbooks' monthly *Small Press Review* (incorporating *Small Magazine Review*) and Burning Press's *Taproot Reviews: news and reviews from the micropress underground* both specialize in poetry and fiction (though they do include some non-literary publishers and periodicals).

There is no shortage of directories and review journals dedicated to small press fiction and poetry. Dustbooks' *Directory of Poetry Publishers* details over 2000 publishers. *Light's List* contains names and addresses of over 600 small press magazines (and is extremely cheap), with a brief indication of the topics and genres published in each. *Small Presses and Little Magazines of the UK and Ireland: an address list*, compiled by Peter Finch, although including a handful of generalist alternative publishers, is mostly concerned with new creative writing.

Mail art

Mail art – art that is sent through the postal system – is possibly the most democratic form of artistic expression. Typically one person or organization plans an exhibition (either general or on a specified theme) and calls for art to be sent through the post. This can mean postcards, rubber stamp art, 'conceptual mail', booklets, letters, posters and collages. There tends to be no judging of submissions; all are usually exhibited. All participants ordinarily receive documentation of the exhibition, usually a catalogue. *Global Mail* and *ND* list such calls for work. John Held's *Mail art: an annotated bibliography* is a key source for mail art resources. He is currently preparing a new work, *International networker culture: an annotated bibliography*, which has spawned the irregular periodical *Bibliozine*, each issue documenting his research to date, on the way to its publication in book form.

The Printed Matter Bookstore at Dia's *Books by Artists Catalogue [year]* contains collections of drawings by Sol LeWitt, Fluxus documents and objects from Yoko Ono and George Brecht, artists' periodicals, video and audio recordings, output from mail artists and others whose main medium of expression is the network – be it print, computer or television. Of especial interest are the source books it lists, such as Joan Lyons's *Artists' books: a critical anthology and sourcebook*. One of the publishers featured in the Printed Matter catalogue is Coracle Press, whose *The artist publisher* is a fine introduction to this area of 'self-publishing as a critical alternative' (to borrow the title of the opening section) to the dominance of the fine art world. There are sections on artists' manifestos; magazines, journals and newspapers; artists' and gallery presses; Fluxus; mail art; rubber stamp art.

Music

Just as the readers of science fiction were the pioneers of the fanzines, in music the independent scene was founded by rock and jazz fans, unable to read of their favourite recordings in the mainstream press (many fans went on to found record labels – as did the musicians themselves when the recording contracts dried up). Information about access to cheap record pressing plants and distributors was circulated widely; the production process was demystified – Scritti Politti's early singles always featured a breakdown of the record's costs, right down to the price of the labels, alongside addresses and phone numbers of the cheapest and best. For those without the money to pay for their own records, there was always home recording and duplication on cassette. This has remained part of the alternative music scene ever since, becoming a global network in its own right. It is extensively described in Robin James's *Cassette mythos*.

Maximumrockandroll and Grim Humour fill their pages with record reviews which, whilst taking much from whatever the current hardcore punk scene is concerned with, also cover jazz, electronic music and other cultural emissions such as film, video and books, along with other zines. Exuberant, funny, at times outrageously outspoken (in the spirit of zine culture), both demonstrate with ease how complacently narrow the 'angry' writings of the commercial music press have become. To read their columns is to learn of music entirely removed from Top Forty FM, but there is so much of it that you wonder that you've not heard any of it before. The answer is – as a reaction to what amounts to a mass media blackout – fans and musicians have created their own scene, using their own networks for record distribution and touring. There are hundreds of zines that offer briefer, more specialized versions of these two which are exhaustively reviewed in *Factsheet 5* and *Bypass*.

Maximumrockandroll have also been instrumental in the publication of *Book your own fuckin' life: do it yourself resource guide*. For punks, whether musicians, listeners, anyone involved in punk music, this is the directory for them. It aims to cover all countries to enable bands to arrange their own tours and for fans and musicians to network. It lists under each country bands, record labels, promoters and venues, radio stations, record and book shops and zines. Predictably for a US directory, two-thirds is taken up by a state-by-state guide to that country, and coverage of other countries is patchy. England warrants a mere six pages and lists only 28 bands and three record shops! (Scotland fares even worse.) Since the compilers rely on information contributed by the people 'out there', they are at the mercy of what they receive: their contacts are clearly more extensive in the US.

SAF is one of the few small publishers of music titles. It has published monographs on musicians working at the fringes of popular music such as the Residents, Can and Wire. It is unusual that there are so few book publishers in this field outwith the mainstream – the only other of note is Independent Music Press, publisher of biographies of the Mission, Ned's Atomic Dustbin and Napalm Death. It is fortunate that such is the fans' desire to read about their idols that most of these publications – in contradistinction to most coverage of alternative presses – are reviewed in the mainstream music press.

As new musics arise, so do the publications to support them. The rave culture has already spawned a number of magazines that have become news-stand stalwarts in short order (*DJ* and *Mixmag* are but two), yet there is no shortage of independent magazines covering this field. *Underground News* and *Alien Underground* cover techno, house and ambient musics from all over the world. *ND* and *MFTEQ* (formerly *Music from the Empty Quarter*) take in electronic music of all breeds, from all countries in extensive reviews (as well as providing a mail order service for hard-to-find and small distribution record releases).

Comic art

As with fiction and poetry, there are now hundreds of self-produced comics. The easiest way into this area is through the review zines. In common with much of the material it reviews, *Zum!* is a carefully crafted labour of love – mostly hand-lettered and illustrated, its pages often resemble those of a comic. It is well illustrated from the comics themselves and its reviews are lengthy, detailed and fair. *Indy* is at the professional end of comic review journals, providing as much news and interviews as it does reviews of the comics themselves. Again, as all comic reviews should be, it is extremely well-illustrated from the comics themselves. Although *Zum!* and *Indy* hardly exhaust the range of comic reviews, they are useful places to start, with little duplication between them. And as with many alternative review journals in the arts, editors and reviewers speak from a great deal of personal knowledge, since they are all involved in comic creation themselves.

References

1. Cited by Edward Herman in *Beyond Hypocrisy: decoding the news in an age of propaganda* (Boston, Mass.: South End Press, 1992), p. 17.
2. Donald Rooum, *What is Anarchism?* (London: Freedom Press, 1993), p. 1.
3. Bob Black, 'A Situationist bibliography' in *Beneath the underground* (Portland, Oregon: Feral House, 1994), pp. 100–104.
4. It is at present illegal to import *EIDOS* into the UK, although a few individuals have succeeded in receiving copies through the post. Despite the bulk of its pages being taken up with the printed word – erotic poetry and fiction, letters and those extensive book reviews, UK Customs and Excise have

declared it obscene on the basis of a few small photographs in its classified advertisements.

5. Chris Dodge, 'Alternative sex: some 'zines, comics, books, and sources', *Collection Building* **13**(1), 1993, pp. 48–51. Reprinted in *Alternative Library Literature: 1992–1993*, edited by Sanford Berman and James Danky (Jefferson, NC: McFarland, 1994), pp. 332–5.

6. *Manufacturing consent: Noam Chomsky and the media*, edited by Mark Achbar (Montreal: Black Rose Books, 1994), p. 184.

3 The Subjects of Alternative Literature – Critiques of Public Life and the Mass Media

How the mass media shapes information

The distorting influence of all mass media has been demonstrated for many years in the work of people such as Noam Chomsky, John Pilger and the Glasgow University Media Group. Their books have been published by mainstream publishers such as Routledge, Verso and Pluto, yet their ideas hardly have the currency that one would expect of work rigorously sustained for so many years. *The Guardian* is the only newspaper to cover the work of the Glasgow University Media Group on anything like a regular basis (here regular means once a year at best). Pilger has an occasional column in *New Statesman and Society* plus the very occasional feature in *The Guardian*. Chomsky is the author of dozens of books, some published by mainstream publishers, many by the alternatives. But the bulk of his articles appear in the alternative press. The amount of time given on television to dissident and critical views of the media on radio is negligible; on television it is virtually non-existent. The screening of Peter Wintonick and Mark Achbar's film *Manufacturing consent: Noam Chomsky and the media* on Channel 4 in 1993 was unique, even by that channel's standards of critical reporting. In this film Chomsky identifies a number of ways in which the mass media operate:

1. By selecting topics.
2. By emphasis.
3. By the framing of issues.
4. By filtering information.
5. By the bounding of debate.

By these methods, he avers, the mass media determine, select, shape, control and restrict what we see and hear. Consequently what we are able to find out about the world is highly mediated by these practices. There are reasons for this, concretized by Herman and Chomsky in their book *Manufacturing Consent: the political economy of the mass media* as five 'filters' they identify that the media consistently exhibit and that seriously affect the nature and extent of information we are offered.

1. Concentrated ownership and power.
2. The influence of advertising as the primary source of income for the mass media.
3. The reliance on information provided by government, business and 'experts'.
4. 'Flak', meaning negative responses to media items, especially as orchestrated by powerful interests.
5. Anti-communism or anti-left-wing bias.

The upshot of these filters has two major impacts that are crucial to our understanding of the range and the importance of alternative publishing, particularly as a counter and a complement to the mass media. These are political bias and commercial bias. Both consistently squeeze out certain topics from mainstream discussion. The first is especially important and deserves looking at in some depth, since it has an impact not only on politics but on how we are encouraged to see the world from all perspectives: national, social, cultural and political. Such a narrowing of perspective has grave implications for our education and for democracy, and consequently for the information that is made available in our libraries. It is appropriate therefore to consider it in detail. There follow three examples of that narrowing of perspective: in home news, foreign news and in commercial bias, with indications of how the alternative press can provide complementary information.

Political bias in the media: the case of Northern Ireland

Within the limits of mainstream politics certain topics are routinely reported in remarkably partial ways. In 1994 the broadcasting ban on Sinn Fein was lifted. So ended six years of political censorship that has become the norm for our television and radio stations. No live debates or live questioning have taken place for six years. We have seen only pre-recorded, dubbed interviews. On radio the situation has been worse: a dubbed radio interview is no interview at all. During the Ban, coverage such as this was typical: 'What is Gerry Adams without a bomb?' asked one reporter. Adams was described as using 'verbal bullying ... wild analogy, evasion, contradiction and intransigence: the verbal equivalent of terrorism'. No other leader of a British political party has ever been described in such terms.[1] Tony Hall, managing director of BBC news and current affairs, declared: 'Broadcasters do their best to present a fair and full picture of the events in Northern Ireland, but there is always the danger that the logistics of reporting within the terms of the Notice will inhibit our journalism.'[2] Yet the style of reporting in our newspapers had little to do with the Ban.

The ceasefire declaration by the IRA provides a useful case study of how the mass media have set an effectively anti-Republican agenda and stuck to it for some 25 years (at least). This is especially noticeable in the national daily newspapers, where the ceasefire was greeted with in-depth, multi-page coverage. It is not appropriate here to examine all the papers in depth, so the coverage of the story in *The Independent* of 1 September 1994 must stand for them all. (Those interested will find that the paradigm demonstrated by this paper will be confirmed in the others.) *The Independent* also provided the most extensive coverage: eight pages and an editorial. A patronizing , uncomprehending picture was drawn by Andrew Marr, who claimed that 'Ulster will re-enter modern times and ... politics will come to be about hospitals, training programmes and environmentalism, not dead kings and rival theologies'. Conor Cruise O'Brien was firmly negative. In a piece entitled 'This is not peace; it is simply the prelude to a different war', he talked slyly of the 'IRA (aka Sinn Fein)' and how its 'unarmed struggle ... will dominate the period of the ceasefire, and is intended to speed up the destabilisation [of Northern Ireland]'. He does not reveal his no doubt unimpeachable source for such a bold assertion.

The only view that is at all supportive of the Republicans is that of Ken Livingstone. His view accorded roughly one sixty-fourth of the paper's coverage. Indeed, his is the only pro-Republican voice to be heard in any of the broadsheet newspapers of this day, the only person to consider that those who might 'wreck this latest chance' for peace might in fact be amongst the loyalist paramilitaries, not the IRA. This appears too radical a sentiment to be accorded anything like equal treatment with the majority of the coverage, which plays down or simply ignores this threat. Livingstone's view is of course not the dominant one: it is founded on the belief that the situation in Northern Ireland is a direct result of centuries of British imperialism and that it is not simply – as is typically reported – the consequence of two religious communities at war.

If we are not to find representative views of all sides within the mainstream press it is clear that we must look elsewhere, for however partial other sources might be, they will at least provide us with information and comment to supplement what we can easily find. Partisan newspapers and magazines become crucial: the Republican version of events will always be found in the weekly *An Phoblacht* (*Republican News*) and magazines such as *An Camcheachta* (*The Starry Plough*) and *Troops Out*. The Sinn Fein

Book Bureau Catalogue is an obvious source of economic and political analyses from the Republican point of view of a thoroughness that is not found in mainstream publications. Critiques of the media representation of Northern Ireland will be found most notably in the catalogue of Pluto Press, including Liz Curtis's *Ireland: the propaganda war* and David Miller's *Don't mention the war: Northern Ireland, propaganda and the media*.

Foreign news reporting from a single viewpoint: the case of East Timor

In 1975, Indonesia invaded East Timor. In the same year Pol Pot's genocide in Cambodia began. Both continued for the next three years, resulting in over 200 000 dead in East Timor and a comparable figure in Cambodia. Media estimates vary wildly from tens of thousands to millions but, according to US officials themselves, the US carpet bombing of Cambodia of 1969–75 left 600 000 dead and it was estimated that one million would die from hunger and disease. Although these are comparable atrocities, media coverage of Cambodia was far in excess of that of East Timor for the period 1975–1979.[3]

In similar fashion the UK's involvement in East Timor has been played down by the media. We only have the John Pilger articles in *New Statesman and Society* and *The Guardian* to provide any context. The only truly mass coverage of East Timor came immediately pre-invasion when it gained independence from Portugal in 1974. Here the concern was the threat of newly independent countries and Russian influence over the fragmenting Portuguese empire. Coverage dropped after that to a much lower level, where it has remained, focusing on economic interest above all.

Noam Chomsky has said of the *Financial Times*: 'That's the only paper that tells the truth.'[4] What he means is that in a world of information where most papers pretend to a fair and balanced coverage, free from all explicit bias, the *Financial Times* is one of the few papers that publishes explicitly on behalf of a special class – the business interest. The paper looks at the world on their terms, using concepts familiar to them, discussing the issues that are properly at the heart of geopolitics: commerce and industry. When Indonesia hosted the Asia Pacific Economic Co-operation (APEC) summit in 1994, the régime of General Suharto was examined closely by the paper. But the reports were less interested in the continuing human rights abuses perpetrated by Indonesia in East Timor than in the potential for trade. When the paper described Suharto as an 'unlikely champion of free trade', it wasn't the 200 000 dead in East Timor that warranted such hesitation but his protectionist interests over trade. The interest shown in East Timor by the US and the UK has nothing to do with repression and murder, and everything to do with the gas and oil fields that lie off its coast. 'Exxon sign Indonesian natural gas field accord' was an especially important outcome of the APEC summit. In all some '$40 billion worth of contracts and memoranda of understanding' were signed between the US and Indonesia. Arms sales remain high, and here the *Financial Times* reports a Pentagon spokesman in extremely lucid mode: 'The basic reason for selling weapons overseas has been to advance our foreign policy goals. It will remain to advance our foreign policy goals.'

There is, however, no shortage of information about the human rights situation in East Timor. Organizations such as TAPOL (the Indonesia human rights campaign), the British Coalition for East Timor (BCET) and the East Timor Action Network produce regular bulletins on events there. BCET's bi-monthly newsletter *East Timor: it's time to talk* provides a regular update of events in East Timor in its struggle against the Indonesian government. A lead article provides news and analysis on the current situation in advance of the mainstream media. BCET also distributes *East Timor: an Indonesian intellectual speaks out*, a collection of essays and an interview with George Aditjondro, one of the leaders of the Indonesian movement in support of East Timor.

Commercial bias in the media: the case of McDonald's

In the UK the most striking example of commercial bias in the media in recent years has been the so called 'McLibel' trail, in which two members of London Greenpeace stand accused of publishing and distributing a leaflet containing defamatory statements about McDonald's, claiming that the company is responsible, *inter alia*, for the destruction of rainforests to provide land for beef cattle, infringing workers' rights, cruelty to animals and promoting unhealthy eating. The defendants are unemployed, not eligible for legal aid and are therefore conducting their own defence. A better example of David and Goliath it would be hard to find. In fact, this is the first time that individuals have been taken to court by a multinational company: it has happened to organizations before, but not to individuals. Yet reporting on the case has been very low key in the British media (virtually non-existent on television and radio).

It may be argued that the reason for this lack of coverage is commercial pressure. McDonald's is a major advertiser across all the mass media and during the trial appeared to double its efforts to promote itself as the innocent party, even publishing and distributing its own leaflet through its restaurants, branding the accused as liars. The presence of McDonald's in the mass media reached unprecedented proportions in the autumn of 1994 with an article in *The Guardian* (23 September) extolling the virtues of fast-food chains, illustrated throughout (and in colour on the front page of its tabloid section) with photographs of McDonald's restaurants and products. This reached remarkable proportions with an eight-page supplement in *The Times* (30 September) 'celebrating' 20 years of McDonald's in the UK. This comprised a handful of articles written by staff writers and freelancers purporting to be objective in reporting about aspects of the company. The bulk of the supplement contained pages of advertising for McDonald's and all its supply and service companies.

Apart from one article in *New Statesman and Society*, published well into the trial, there has been little critical comment at all from the mainstream press. Neither has there been much information on the progress of the trial, or even its background. Turn to the alternative press, unworried by alienating potential multinational advertisers, and we find the most detailed coverage and comment imaginable outwith the legal journals. London Greenpeace themselves have published regular updates on the progress of the trial, including a lengthy summary of the proceedings. Every environmental, anarchist and animal rights, anti-consumerist newspaper and journal in the UK has reported on it regularly. The same can be said of our other 'counter sources' on Northern Ireland and Indonesia. But since none of the publications in which these views appear is indexed or abstracted anywhere, the views and information remain within a small group of people. Anyone who is not a part of the networks within which these publications circulate would have to be a fanatic to find them. Under such conditions of marginal existence, dissident views such as these will quickly disappear.

Alternative sources for media criticism

So far, this chapter has drawn much on the work of Noam Chomsky and Edward Herman. They are not the only people working in this field but they are certainly two of its most outspoken and prolific researchers. Their jointly authored *Manufacturing consent: the political economy of the mass media* contains the major exposition of their thesis. Subsequent works by them individually have added further weight to this. Chomsky is especially prolific, but his major addition to this field is *Necessary illusions: thought control in democratic societies*. The briefer works *Letters from Lexington: reflections on propaganda* and *Media control: the spectacular achievements of propaganda* are excellent introductions to the thesis. Herman's book *Beyond hypocrisy: decoding the news in an age of propaganda* is also worth reading, especially for its 'Doublespeak dictionary' of terms commonly used by the mass media and politicians. Martin A. Lee's *Unreliable sources: a guide to detecting bias in news media* and

Eleanor MacLean's *Between the lines: how to detect bias and propaganda in the media and everyday life* provide materials that would be of great value for classroom study of these topics. A number of magazines and journals are dedicated to the task of analysing and decoding the messages of the mass media. All present their ideas in a readable, accessible style, often humorously, nevertheless maintaining a critical rigour (a combination that is common in alternative literature).

Extra! (published bi-monthly by Fairness and Accuracy in Reporting (FAIR)) casts its net wide to include electronic as well as paper media. It has provided rigorous and valuable insights – unavailable elsewhere – of the reporting of Desert Storm and has devoted many of its pages to environmental reporting. In its own words: 'FAIR focuses public awareness on the narrow corporate ownership of the press, the media's allegiance to official agendas and their insensitivity to women, labor, minorities and other public interest constituencies.' *Propaganda Review* is more concerned with the use of language, phrasing and structure to exclude significant sections of the population, to limit the bounds of debate and to prevent discussion of anything but the most familiar topics. It examines the hidden agendas that politicians and journalists reveal through their use of what, in *The Fine Art of Propaganda*, Alfred and Elizabeth Lee called 'the seven propaganda devices', commonly used by professional propagandists to persuade their audience that they have a monopoly on the truth. An excellent digest of the devices, using George Bush's State of the Union address of 1991, is to be found in Jeanine Olson's article, 'The Seven Propaganda Devices' in *Propaganda Review*.[5]

Although 1994 saw its final issue, for many years in its monthly coverage *Lies of Our Times* (subtitled 'a magazine to correct the record') exposed the bias, inaccuracies and false premises of the *New York Times* in particular and the US printed media in general. Its recent issues focused on East Timor, systematically ignored by most of the US media, the continuing bias against Palestinians and the record of anti-environmentalist reporting still prevalent, even this long after Rio. Every year Project Censored produce a compilation of the 'top twenty-five' stories that its researchers feel have been played down or ignored by the mainstream media. *Censored!: the news that didn't make the news ... and why* has covered 'the real news' in Somalia, Haiti and Cuba, as well as looking at items closer to home such as drugs, the poor and minority rights. *Adbusters Quarterly* is a glossy magazine that specializes in designing and publishing parodies of current major advertising campaigns. It is especially well-known for its versions of Calvin Klein's 'Obsession' and Absolut Vodka, at the same time as it reports on the encroach-ment of advertising into such areas as public education (Burger King Academies and other schools funded by corporations such as Whittle Communications and McDonald's). This subversion of advertising has led to the portmanteau term 'subvertising' to describe advertisements altered or redesigned to make a social or political point, usually highlighting the activities of the busi-ness or product being advertised. Although there are no such single-issue journals in the UK (due largely to economies of scale), media control is still discussed, but as part of a wider con-cern for current affairs. There are, however, a small number of pamphlets and books that combine the critical rigour of Chomsky and Herman with the exuberance and audacity of *Adbusters Quarterly*. *Test card F: television, mythinformation and social control* and *TV Times: a seven day guide to killing your TV* are two of the best examples, their anonymous authors employing collage, cut-up text and commentary to produce brief works that have an immediacy and a power rarely found even in more sus-tained works. All such interventions, subvertising, radical com-mentaries on the media, and the potential of the alternative media themselves to create unmediated news and information services are examined briefly yet authoritatively by Mark Dery in *Culture jamming: hacking, slashing and sniping in the empire of signs*.

Alternative current affairs reporting

Free from the restrictions of reporting required by the British 'lobby' system and the institution of 'D' notices, untrammelled by the nexus of concentrated ownership and commercial control, the reporters and writers of the alternative press can afford to research stories that do not have as their primary aim the sale of newspapers and that do not have to fit in with a key advertiser's motives. They do not even have to lead to front page news, and they can be commented upon to a depth that most of the mass media would find unacceptable. In countries that have become, in recent decades, as Edward Herman has it, 'notable for increased secrecy, the curtailment of access to information, covert operations, deception, and manipulation of the press',[6] it is fitting that the substantial investigative work exposing these tendencies should come from the very alternative media that is so many times marginalized, ignored and ridiculed by the mainstream.

Newspapers

There is currently no such thing as an alternative daily newspaper in either the UK or the US. Michael Albert of *Z Magazine* has recommended the launching of a national alternative weekly newspaper for the US which would integrate the existing expertise and resources of many already involved in the production of their own (less frequent) newspapers and magazines. This has caused concern in some quarters, since it is felt it would diminish the diversity and pluralism that is at the heart of alternative publishing.

This diversity remains, however, and there are many alternative newspapers (of varying frequency) to be found. The most prominent of these are published by political parties and groups, usually espousing some variant of Marxism-Leninism or Trotskyism. In these you may still find headlines such as 'Lenin's materialism and empirio-criticism today – see centre pages' (from a recent copy of *The Newsline*, the daily newspaper of the Workers Revolutionary Party). All such publications are of limited use to provide alternative perspectives or news unheard elsewhere, since their doctrinaire approach is more interested in recycling mainstream news, ascribing each strike or workers' action to the power of their cause or ideology. Such papers survive only due to funding from the relevant parties. (The occasional critical journal *Trotwatch* and its even more occasional pamphlets provide an entertaining and investigative commentary on these parties and their publications.) The one exception is *The Morning Star*, which does contain analysis and reporting that is more than mere dogma. Indeed, it is the only daily newspaper in the UK that consistently reports on Northern Ireland and Cuba from 'the other side', providing much information and commentary that would otherwise be lost.

There are a number of newspapers that cover issues from anarchist and libertarian perspectives and which provide information on issues that are either ignored or marginalized by the mass media. The long-standing fortnightly *Freedom* provides the most regular summary of national and international anarchist news. *Counter Information* is a four-page quarterly, gathering news from all over the world about people's struggles, exploring the similarities in local situations in places as apparently disparate as Edinburgh and Calcutta. Its abiding interests lie in documenting the struggle against racism and fascism and the establishment of community solidarity groups throughout the world, but emphatically on a local level, involving direct participation. *Contraflow* is the British arm of the European Counter Network and looks mostly at Britain (its calendar of events and actions exclusively so). It is a useful networking tool, listing many names and addresses as well as acting as a barometer of the current concerns of anarchist groups. Both *Counter Information* and *Contraflow* are distributed free of charge.

In the UK there is a preponderance of local weekly newspapers that, whilst providing a little community information and superficial local news coverage, function mainly as advertising space. But we should not forget the value of alternative and independent local newspapers. These are especially strong in the US, with such titles as the local anarchist paper *The Blast!* examining Twin Cities (Minneapolis and St. Paul) news in national and international contexts. In the UK these are rarer and less frequent. An example close to home is Edinburgh's free newssheet *The Stockbridge and Newtown Rocket*, produced by the Stockbridge and New Town Solidarity Network, which reports from a radical perspective on local and national government issues affecting residents.

Alternative radio and television

Alternative journalism on radio and television is a rare beast indeed, since access to the technology is even more mediated than access to mass printing technology. Public access radio and television in the US has, however, led to the rise of a small number of programmes. For those of us without access to the broadcasts themselves, some of these are available on tape. David Barsamian's Alternative Radio series of cassettes are copies of interviews with such critics of the mass media and US government policy as Noam Chomsky, Ben Bagdikian, Edward Herman and Edward Said. A number of Barsamian's interviews have also been published, notably the collection *Stenographers to power: media and propaganda*, featuring, amongst others, interviews with Noam Chomsky, Ben Bagdikian, Alexander Cockburn, Erwin Knoll (the editor of *The Progressive)* and Jeff Cohen (Executive Director of FAIR). His collections of interviews with Chomsky (*Chronicles of Dissent* and *Keeping the rabble in line*) and with Said (*The pen and the sword*) are also simple and persuasive introductions to their philosophies.

Paper Tiger Television makes available its investigative programmes on the mass media and the communications industry on video, and now has a catalogue of over 200 30-minute programmes available, examining advertisements, news gathering, international politics and the treatment of women, children and ethnic minorities on television.

Current affairs magazines and other commentaries

Whilst magazines such as *Dissent* and *The Progressive* provide regular comment and analysis their approach is more in line with that of the mainstream political journals, not in their content and viewpoints, but in their intellectual weight. Their widespread distribution throughout the US and their appearance on newsstands and in bookshops gives them a profile not available to most alternatives. On the other hand, the fortnightly *In These Times* and the monthly *Z Magazine*, key alternative current affairs journals in the US, provide in-depth articles on topics that are consistently played down or ignored by the mass media. Their frequency and constancy (both rare in alternative publishing) enables them to provide current and thoroughgoing critical analysis and comment on current world events in which the US has a major part, both domestic and international. In Canada *This Magazine* examines political and cultural issues in a popular style, yet many of its feature articles and ideas go well beyond the internal politics of that country. It is especially strong on censorship issues, sexual politics and education. The *Open Magazine Pamphlet Series* comprises talks and reports about aspects of US domestic and foreign policy. These have included Joel Beinin on the Gulf War, Helen Caldicott on environmental imperatives and Rosalyn Baxandall on abortion. Together they form a unique commentary on contemporary issues that have a value well beyond the US. The *Real story series* of pocket books published by Odonian Press presents in clear and simple language overviews of key political topics such as the role of the CIA (*The CIA's greatest hits*), US foreign policy (*What Uncle Sam really wants*) and political assassination (*Who killed JFK?*).

In its first issue *CovertAction Quarterly* described itself as 'a permanent weapon in the fight against the CIA, the FBI, military intelligence, and all the other instruments of US imperialist oppression throughout the world' and was the major US journal for the examination of the activities of the intelligence and security agencies. Former CIA employee John Stockwell has said that it provides 'more information about the complete scope of the national security complex, its myths, rationales, secret wars, media manipulations, and abuses, than anything else in print'.[7] It has now widened its brief significantly, including much more 'overground' political analysis and reporting on those 'other instruments' such as the World Bank, GATT and the IMF, in particular their role in destabilizing the economies of the developing countries. It has also reported extensively on non-US topics such as Russia's avowed 'democratic reforms' and the continuing human rights abuses in Northern Ireland and South Africa and their connections to right-wing funding agencies. *Unclassified* contains critical surveys of the US intelligence scene from former agents and other employees. The latest projects of the World Bank are assessed in *Bankcheck Quarterly*, which also notes the increasing campaigns and protests against activities in the countries of the South and digests international news reporting on the Bank, the IMF and the G7.

In the UK, apart from the newsstand regulars *New Statesman and Society* and *Red Pepper*, there are fewer, less frequent titles, but they do exist. *Here and Now* performs a similar service to *Z Magazine*, from an avowedly anti-authoritarian stance. Its coverage is remarkable – in a single issue it might examine state policing and the privatization of public space, the activities of the security services and the future of work. Its book reviews are occasions for polemics and apologias, never mere textual analysis. It blends a rigorous, academic style with plain speaking – many commentators rate it as unique, the only source for consistently acerbic and informed commentaries on present-day statism. *Casablanca* is the product (we understand) of a number of anonymous, disaffected moonlighting journalists from the liberal left of the British media. If *Casablanca* has an identifiable theme it is the role of politics in culture and about liberating that culture through critical and creative writing and by discussing it on its own terms. *Open Eye* is the UK equivalent to *CovertAction Quarterly*, although it also takes a critical look at the British media as well as examining the activities of the security services. It covers a vast range of topics: free trade, environmental activism, reports from the South by indigenous commentators (a rarity in mainstream media), microwave weapons and other allegations of state terrorism. Despite its irregular appearance it remains the prime source of alternative investigative journalism and research in the UK.

Statewatch is the successor to *State Research*, once the only alternative journal investigating the activities of the British state. *Statewatch* ('monitoring the state and civil liberties in the UK and

Europe') provides a news digest and current awareness service taken from newspapers, national and European governmental documents and the alternative press. Each issue features 'new materials', listing books, pamphlets and journal articles on each topic covered (these include Northern Ireland, immigration, prisons, racism and fascism, security and intelligence). It has also published *Statewatching the new Europe: a handbook on the European state* and makes available back issues of *State Research*.

Parapolitics and deep politics

The work of so-called 'conspiracy theorists' is frequently dismissed as no more than ravings, and as such is marginalized in much the same way that critiques of the media are marginalized, through the very channels of the mass media themselves. Consequently the public are kept unaware of a vast body of knowledge and continuing research into the mechanisms that enable such control to take place. Inevitably much of this work is speculative – the powers that be are hardly likely to open up their procedures and archives to public scrutiny – yet no more speculative than most scientific theories. Postulates are set up and then tested. It is the test of any theory that provides real proof, not any subjective idea of how fanciful it might at first appear. We have seen how Herman and Chomsky's theory of thought control through the mass media has been tested repeatedly and has never been disconfirmed. This does not secure it for all time, but it certainly makes it worthy of consideration and, in the absence of a rival theory, is the best we have.

'Parapolitics' is the term most frequently applied to the analysis of political institutions in order to discover whether there exist such hidden mechanisms of control. The majority of the primary research takes place in alternative literature. Parapolitics has been defined by Peter Dale Scott, one of the foremost researchers in this field, as 'a system or practice of politics in which accountability is consciously diminished'. But parapolitics, he avers, is but one occurrence of what he calls 'deep politics', meaning 'all those political practices, deliberate or not, which are usually repressed rather than acknowledged'.[8] We should note how this differs from the accepted meaning of conspiracy theory, where all such activity is considered both covert *and* deliberate. Peter Dale Scott's definition of deep politics allows for the irrational and unquantifiable. This has two effects: whilst it undoubtedly complicates any research project, it does at least encourage a rigorous, critical approach to that research, since it warns the researcher against looking for deliberateness in every action of every governmental agency.

The alleged 'shoot to kill' policy of the British Army and the Royal Ulster Constabulary in Northern Ireland is an example of parapolitical practice, since it refers to a policy that has been consciously designed for a specific end, and its existence suppressed (this is assuming it to be true). By contrast the British Army's alleged collusion with Loyalist paramilitary forces is not parapolitical, since any examination of this relationship not only encompasses policy decisions but the accidental effects of organized crime on arms shipments. This takes us out of the realm of political arrangements and into the more unpredictable systems of sociopolitical studies encapsulated by the phrase 'deep politics'.

Lobster is a splendid example of a parapolitical journal. Or rather, *Lobster are* a splendid example, since following an editorial split there are now two journals of that name. The net result of the split is twice as much research into a field that is mostly ignored by the mainstream press. Both are worth investigating for their research on MI5, MI6 and other covert state activities, research that is largely unavailable elsewhere. While Steve Dorril's *Lobster* concentrates on the activities of the British and US security services, Robin Ramsay's *Lobster* casts its net wider to encompass histories of fascism, the JFK assassination, the Lockerbie bombing and the military's medical experiments on service personnel. What both *Lobsters* excel at are finding the links between apparently unrelated events, or finding the significance of an event that many commentators would consider trivial.

The majority of this research does not take place in an academic setting; it is undertaken by amateurs, yet its nature is far from amateurish. Since so little kudos attaches to such work, there are none of the pressures that academics are frequently influenced by, such as publishing to improve their academic standing or that of their institution. 'Many people have an impression that so-called "conspiracy" researchers make a lot of money with their research. This for the most part is not true ... there are hundreds of independent efforts paid for with the blood, sweat and money of the researchers. They produce their wares more for the sake of sharing some previously undiscovered truth or some new perspective to a larger community.'[9] Its research practices do, however, borrow much from the best of academic research: their articles are always well-referenced, and the researchers ensure that the thesis they are developing is documented at every stage (nowhere is the art of the footnote better practised or more finely wrought than in the pages of *Lobster*). This has a value for the librarian as well as the researcher, beyond the obvious 'academic respectability' that tends to accrue to such practices, since it means that the research itself can function as a partial bibliography to its field of enquiry.

Periodicals such as *Steamshovel Press*, *Paranoia* and *Flatland* investigate the more extreme ends of conspiracy theory, which we should not ignore if we are to truly represent the scope of parapolitical and conspiracy literature. As the compiler of the New Paradigms Project (a database of conspiracy research) warns, 'The books, reports, and articles included are not without serious faults. Most are guilty of blatant partisan bias ... We suggest many authors not for objective information, but for insight into all possible viewpoints on a subject.' Amongst the extreme speculation will be found many nuggets of broader relevance thrown up in the forays into the covert sides of government and corporate interest. Every article in *Flatland* is accompanied by extensive sidebars of further reading, mostly taken from the alternative press. All the titles may be ordered from *Flatland*'s mail-order catalogue. In the UK, C. G. H. Services produce a comparable catalogue, with an emphasis on scholarly research. Many of the titles in their list are extracted from bibliographies and reviews in *Lobster*, *Statewatch* and *Capital and Class*.

Dave Emory's *Archive cassette catalog* is a parapolitical, conspiracy theorist's version of Barsamian's *Alternative radio*. Emory is a political researcher who broadcasts on college radio, making his shows available on cassette. Typical subjects are the assassination of JFK and the involvement of the US government and its agencies in covert fascism.

Alternative reference sources

Since much of what appears in alternative publishing is the result of investigative journalism, it should come as no surprise to find that the reference works that alternative publishing produces are far more than straightforward assemblages of facts and figures, although their sources might well lie in the public domain. Indeed, such works show us how much information is already available to us, were we only to have time to collate and edit it. We already depend on organizations such as Dun and Bradstreet and the Confederation of British Industry to provide the 'objective' mainstream view of commerce and industry, drawn from annual reports and other documents in the public domain, but we can also rely on the alternative press to trawl those same public sources to provide supplementary information: the less flattering, more critical side of many business activities. What follows is a selection to indicate the breadth of such alternative reference sources.

The Greenpeace guide to anti-environmental organisations by Carl Deal lists over 50 US-based public relations firms, think tanks, foundations, endowments and charities that are used by commerce and industry to discredit and attack environmental groups and their members. The activities of such organizations, their backers, sources of funding and office-bearers are all detailed, accompanied by comprehensive sources for all the facts and quotations from which the book has been compiled. Equally scrupulous in detailing its sources is *Ethical Consumer*, which might be thought of as the *Which?* magazine of the socially responsible shopper. Its meticulous research amongst all the available evidence in the public domain makes it the only updating service about the ethical and environmental impacts of the activities and products of commerce and industry. These are gathered under headings such as human rights, employment rights, irresponsible marketing, political donations and animal rights. Its thorough sourcing makes it a reliable research tool for those interested in finding out more about companies than is in their annual reports. *Ethical Consumer* also makes this research available as an on-line service known as *Corporate Responsibility On-Line*. The *Scum Directory* is the nearest we have to a British version of *The Greenpeace guide to anti-environmental organisations*, but it could not be more different. Rather than a perfect bound paperback book, it presently comprises a mere seven, unpaginated, single-sided sheets (it makes no claim to comprehensiveness). This is an animal rights activist's reference work – updated every three months – to British companies that are part of the meat and fish industries, that use vivisection or that are otherwise engaged in or supportive of animal rights abuses.

The Arms Traders examines another activity of business that is of great ethical and humanitarian concern throughout the world. The lists here cover the countries of the UK only, with county lists for England. The arms trade is notoriously secretive and this is compounded by the scattered and often disinformative material found in the public domain. *The Arms Traders* is compiled from works such as the *Jane's* series, company annual reports, catalogues of arms exhibitions and the investigative resources of such bodies as the Ethical Investment Research Service and the Stockholm International Peace Research Institute.

A Who's Who of the British Secret State was compiled by Steve Dorril, one of the editors of *Lobster*. It comprises almost 2 000 biographical entries, the product of, in its editor's words, 'long hours of tedious research in the local reference library'. Dorril draws on the work of such writers as Nigel West (Rupert Allason), Chapman Pincher and Roger Faligot, as well as well-known sources such as the Diplomatic Lists, *Who's Who* and *The Times Obituaries* to bring together for the first time (and last? – there has been no second edition) details of many previously unrecognized agents. Daniel Brandt and Steve Badrich of Public Information Research have gone one stage further, making their 'who's who of the covert state' available on floppy disks.

Namebase (as it is called) currently contains 142 000 citations on some 67 000 names of those allied to US intelligence, military, diplomatic and corporate activities in the field of covert action (particularly in counterinsurgency operations in other countries). The database enables users to search for references to all names associated with a specific country during a specific year (or a number of years) and can also produce graphs showing the distribution of entries per year over the last 60 years for any listed country.

References

1. Catherine Bennett, 'Apostle of the bullet and the ballot box', *The Guardian*, 4 February 1991, p. 19.
2. Tony Hall, 'Why the broadcasting ban should go', *Index on Censorship*, 8 & 9, 1993, p. 4.
3. Source: *Manufacturing consent: Noam Chomsky and the media*, edited by Mark Achbar (Montreal: Black Rose Books, 1994), pp. 103–107.
4. Ibid., p. 127.
5. Jeanine Olson, 'The Seven Propaganda Devices', *Propaganda Review*, (10), 1993, pp. 18–21, 57–60. The seven propaganda devices were first identified in Alfred McClung Lee and Elizabeth Briant Lee, *The Fine Art of Propaganda* (Harcourt, Brace and Co., 1939. Reprinted: International Society for General Semantics, 1979).
6. Edward Herman, *Beyond Hypocrisy: decoding the news in an age of propaganda* (Boston, Massachusetts: South End, 1992) p. 16.
7. Quoted in *Open Eye* (1), 1991, p.52.
8. All quotes are from a review of his *Deep Politics and the Death of J.F.K.* by William Clark, *Here and Now* (15), p. 28.
9. Ken Thomas, editor of Steamshovel Press, quoted in 'Steamshovel sued', *Steamshovel Press*, (10), 1994, p. 59.

4 Obstacles to Acquiring Alternative Literature

Selection and censorship in libraries

There have been very few comprehensive or reliable surveys of librarians' attitudes to censorship. Two of the most revealing appeared last year, the first as part of the UK's Department of National Heritage's *Review of the Public Library Service in England and Wales*, in a section headed 'Books, reading and censorship'.[1] The report claims to have 'discovered differing views on the subject of censorship', yet there is a striking uniformity amongst the attitudes of those surveyed: professional librarians, 'other library staff', users and non-users. Although the survey finds chief executives of local authorities to be 'firmly against all forms of censorship', one of the two quotes (intended to be representative) is in favour of banning (or continuing to ban) soft porn from libraries, whilst the other defines censorship in terms of librarians 'around five or ten years ago ... pander[ing] to their own social consciences' and banning racist and sexist materials.

The remainder of this section of the report (three pages) is taken up by a series of spider plots, indicating the respondents'

attitudes towards a range of materials. Most of the categories –
and they are categories, not specific titles – tend to areas that are
uncontroversial in any fundamental way in the 1990s: sex education, AIDS education and other types of 'sensitive materials'
('sensitive' is left undefined). The majority of users and non-
users believe that 'items containing offensive language' (there is
no definition of 'offensive') should not be stocked, whilst the
library staff believe they should be (but only available to adults).
There is unanimous agreement that racist, sexist and ethnically-
biased materials should not be stocked, but there is no mention
of politically or socially controversial literature. In fact when the
survey steps outside the standard discourse of censorship (sex,
rude words, racism, sexism) it flounders. Apparently in an effort
to look at other areas of controversial material, it goes so far as to
posit a category hitherto unknown in any public library: 'Books
on how to make nuclear weapons'. Needless to say, all the
respondents are firmly against these being stocked at all. (There
are enough actual categories that could have been included here
and that would have been far more meaningful – this book is
replete with them.)

The heart of the problem of censorship in the UK is surely that
librarians are not even fully aware of what is available and that
any attempts at censorship are made more from ignorance than
from intent. Perhaps we should be grateful that this situation
pertains in the UK since our other survey – of Southern Africa –
finds librarians in a far more actively repressive role.

Buhle Mbambe, in a paper presented to the 1994 SCECSAL
conference, found that librarians from Zimbabwe and South
Africa felt that there were more positive attributes to censorship
than negative ones, a significant attribute being that state censorship safeguarded libraries from censorship by librarians impos-
ing their own morals on the public! This finding seems to
confirm fears about the innate conservativeness of many librarians, disguised though it may be as professional objectivity: 'One
can only conclude that librarians like, or do not mind, censorship'.[2]

The results of these surveys justify a concern about librarians
bringing their own prejudices to bear on selection decisions at

the same time that an immanent morality is invoked, absolving them from acquiring 'controversial' and 'sensitive' materials. Are these the real reasons behind the lack of alternative materials in libraries? Is it perhaps from a desire to appear objective when selecting materials and looking to a higher moral judge (the state, the employer) for guidance? Given that many alternative materials tend to be considered 'underground', 'subversive' or otherwise undesirable, does it not make the librarian's job easier if they are simply not considered?

According to the standards expected of the professional bodies representing librarians (at least in the US and Britain), the practice of censorship and the restriction of access to information by librarians should never be a problem. The American Library Association's Code of Professional Ethics declares that its members are 'explicitly committed to intellectual freedom and the freedom of access to information' and that 'librarians must resist all efforts by groups or individuals to censor library materials'. The Library Association (UK), whilst declaring that it 'opposes censorship in all its forms' (in its response to the *Report of the PEN Committee on Censorship* on censorship in children's literature), in its 1989 *Policy Statement on Censorship* does allow the librarian 'full discretion over the acquisitions made by the library service'. This is intended to give librarians control independent of their employer, but it does leave the librarian in a position of potential irresponsibility. Elsewhere in the statement, reference is made to providing 'as far as resources allow, all books, periodicals and other materials, *except the trivial*, in which its readers claim *legitimate interest*' (author's emphases). Those two phrases are crucial to many acquisition policies: the plea of 'not enough money' has been used by librarians unwilling to consider stock beyond their standard repertoire and the designation 'trivial' (read: unpopular, unreadable, whatever) may be used to keep the shelves free from subversive writings. (It is hard to know why such a clause was added. Even the LA's Chief Executive admits (in a letter to the author) that he has 'no idea what the authors [of the statement] had in mind when they used the word [trivial]'.)

The setting up and subsequent demonization of a category is common practice in the media, and its effect on the public (and librarians are members of that public, after all) should not be underestimated. The anti-porn moralists who inhabit the tabloid newspapers have no qualms about publishing pornographic literature to show us how corrupting it is (neatly sidestepping the accusation of pandering to the prurient interest). An example is the attraction the British press – both tabloid and broadsheet – had for the graphic details of the letters written by Colin Stagg to a policewoman, who was attempting to incriminate him as a murderer. Yet even his acquittal did not stop the *Sunday People* publishing four pages of his violent, pornographic fiction from these letters. Even the 'quality' papers were not immune from this. *The Guardian* went so far as to demonize the contents of his bookshelf, 'filled with titles such as *The Cult and the Occult; Afterlife; Sixth Sense;* and *Earth Mysteries*'.[3] But are the topics of these books not legitimate areas of interest? Yet by reporting them as the books of an accused murderer (and author of soft porn) they are stigmatized. If librarians are exposed to this enough there is a distinct possibility – as the media is in effect a controlling mechanism – that they will assimilate it as the truth. Then it will be no surprise if their selection decisions become influenced by it, if only out of a misplaced sense of public duty.

'Without a hint of complacency it can be said that censorship is an American rather than a British phenomenon.' This appeared in a book review in a recent issue of *Library Association Record*. It is not a typical statement amongst British librarians, it has to be admitted. More common is the approach of 'the silent majority': silence. That is, either a refusal to engage in the debate about censorship (as being too 'political') or a continuance of the institutional censorship begun by the Victorian library committees. Ian Malley has noted how such routine exclusion of 'left-wing periodical literature' takes place 'as a matter of course'.[4] It is generally accepted within the profession that selection policies should take account of the needs of the communities each library serves. The late 1970s saw the birth of 'community librarianship' by which many librarians sought to make collections and services more responsive and relevant to the needs of the community. They recognized that being responsible for library provision in a multicultural community meant more than merely supplying books and newspapers in languages other than English. Librarians ensured that their stock reflected the cultural and social concerns of the people of the area and helped promote equality of opportunity for groups which had previously been poorly served, or indeed ignored. Librarians became sensitive to the impact of racist and sexist literature on such groups. Such responsiveness to a community's changing needs resulted in procedures which are now commonplace in libraries serving ethnic communities. But to some this was little more than McCarthyism or 'inverted nazism', as one former Brent librarian called it.[5]

Community librarianship was not intended to give librarians licence to impose their own ideology or political bias on a community and its resources. It is about redressing the balance against decades of autocratic selection policies which expressly prevented the public from having any say in what was chosen. On the other hand, professional work that deliberately ignores fundamental aspects of a service may be fairly considered censorship. In 1987 the compilers of the *Northern Ireland Local Studies Bibliography* were accused of censorship when they failed to include political literature in its listings.[6] Ian Malley has remarked that censorship through selection takes place at the hands of right-wing librarians 'quietly and almost subconsciously'.[7] It is not documented how many libraries tacitly 'ban' the *Morning Star* pleading financial constraint rather than political bias – assuming they give any reason at all. (Neither does the *Morning Star* ever appear in the round-up of the morning's lead stories, a feature of many television and radio news magazine programmes.) It is a simple matter to maintain the status quo of a library's collection. This can easily pass unnoticed, yet it may still be called censorship.

External pressures: legal and civil

Alternative titles can be avoided by pleading their seditious or subversive nature. This can be at a legislative level or at the local level of 'the community wouldn't like it'. At the legislative level the most significant example in the UK at the time of writing is the application of Section 28 of the Local Government Act 1988 which explicitly outlaws 'intentionally promoting homosexuality'. As part of local government services, public libraries may well fall foul of the law by displaying literature – otherwise legally published – by or about homosexuals, despite such an injunction contradicting the Public Libraries Act 1964 (requiring every public library to provide 'a comprehensive and efficient service for all persons desiring to make use thereof'). This can even extend to the publication of booklists containing literature about homosexuality. The effects have already been felt in England, with the refusal of Calderdale Library Service to stock the weekly gay and lesbian newspaper *The Pink Paper* after taking legal advice. After pressure from a local HIV prevention group Men on Men and the civil liberties organization Liberty, the library service sought further legal advice. This time the advice was more positive and the publication is now being stocked.[8]

This event raises a number of problems. Firstly it should be noted that prior to 1994 Calderdale Library Service did not stock *The Pink Paper*; it was only at Men on Men's request that the title was even considered, despite it being a nationally-distributed newspaper of some reputation. Since 1988 have libraries begun censoring themselves in the light of Section 28 and refusing to even consider such materials unless pressured so to do? Or may Section 28 be used to plead mitigation for an already existing tacit policy of avoiding 'controversial' materials? Anthony Hugh Thompson has documented the banning of *Soviet News* by a number of local authorities during the Cold War and of the anarchist newspaper *Freedom* by Bristol Public Libraries Committee during the 1960s (local anarchists protesting the latter were reported to the police!).[9] The demonization of anarchists continues today. Recent articles in *Computing* and the *Sunday Times* perpetuated the fallacy that anarchism is equivalent to terrorism, a slander that anarchists have been trying to shake off for over a century and that owes more to the fiction of Joseph Conrad than any contemporary anarchist activity.[10] Such an equation might be seen as giving succour to those who would seek reason to censor anarchist writings (or even non-anarchist publications that are distributed alongside anarchist titles, as feature in AK Distribution's catalogue). Such people might find support in the form of Section 82 of the Criminal Justice and Public Order Act 1994, which makes it a criminal offence to be in possession of articles 'in circumstances which give rise to reasonable suspicion that they are intended for terrorist purposes' and an offence 'to collect or record information which is likely to be of use to terrorists without lawful authority or reasonable excuse for doing so'. Whilst not explicitly naming anarchist groups (or any other groups for that matter), this section is phrased generally enough that it might be interpreted as a type of universal Section 28. Although it is intended to refer to individual possession, it is vague enough in its phrasing that it might just as easily deter libraries from acquiring such materials as they believe might fall under such provisions.

Does bias justify censorship?

Librarians as a profession are alert to the dangers of providing information that misrepresents or distorts, but let us examine two instances of bias in the apparently uncontentious areas of mainstream library provision. Firstly: popular fiction. What dominant representations appear in fiction? Browse round any public library and you will find shelves full of romantic fiction, murder mysteries and westerns; the stock-in-trade of the lending library. Idealized love, unreal romance; glorifications of murder and machismo: all featuring stereotypical, heterosexual characters. Do these not represent bias? Consider that the alternative literature is as replete with fiction as the mainstream and ask yourself: are the standard fiction acquisitions as neutral as we would like to believe?

Now let us turn to non-fiction. Examine the economics books in your local library: are they all not implicitly founded on Keynesian economics, espousing free market ideology as their basis? Do not most of the political titles proceed from the same basis? We find that politics tends to be represented from an economic point of view and that human endeavour and social life is, at bottom, founded on economics and money, rather than on human rights; the dignity of labour, not the dignity of life. Such books tend to fall into three categories: school textbooks (dinning the dominant formulations of past generations into new ears); personal memoirs (of the rich and powerful who have gained success within the dominant paradigm itself); and practical guides to economics (how to evade taxes legally, investing in companies etc.). All reinforce the dominant view from (slightly) different perspectives. What is this outcome, if not biased?

Of course, the alternative publication is also partisan, biased and selective. But it proclaims its selectivity, its bias. On the other hand, most mass media publications are at pains to tell us how impartial and objective they are. The limited space they provide to alternative views, the narrow range of topics permitted for discussion give the strong impression that this is all there is to say. 'If the [mass] media were honest, they would say, Look, here are the interests we represent and this is the framework within which we look at things.'[11] The alternative press provide that honesty, by staking their claim and pledging their allegiance to a cause or a subject or a way of life.

We should not then look for objectivity in alternative publications, nor should we shy away from them because they espouse particular causes. If we are to employ objectivity as a test in acquiring publications or in deciding what titles to investigate, we must apply the same test – just as rigorously – to mainstream publications also. But if we are serious about providing a comprehensive collection of materials then the outlook of any particular title should only matter to us insofar as we are aware that we have acquired material from that perspective and are able to direct users towards it (and if we direct them to it with a caveat regarding its partisan nature, then let us do likewise with our existing mainstream stock).

We must also guard against the proclamation that a 'middle-of-the-road' opinion is somehow 'balanced', that it somehow encompasses all viewpoints (whilst of course judiciously avoiding 'extremist' views). On the contrary, as the Environmental Information Forum has pointed out, the 'middle-of-the-road' opinion:

is just another perspective and shifts as trends in thinking change. It tends to be conservative, consisting of old ideas that have been discussed and are now considered safe. It is also a position that excludes sectors of society other than the dominant social groups.[12]

The myth of the balanced collection

The question of balance frequently arises in relation to the provision of alternative, 'radical' materials in our libraries. Most often this reduces to the 'tit-for-tat' argument, where a librarian will only consider stocking a title if a similar title can be found from the opposite end of the spectrum. This argument has continued to prove effective against the stocking of any 'controversial' materials. But let us look at this argument closely. To begin with, anyone employing it is making the assumption that the item at hand can be located at a precise, objectively defined place along a continuum of views (from 'left' to 'right'). This point may be identified as being a certain distance from the mid-point along the continuum (the centre of the balance). Let this be the 'left' point of view. There must be a corresponding place existing at an equal distance from this mid-point, but on the opposite side. Let this be the 'right' point of view. For every item stocked from the left point of view, it is argued, one must stock an item from the right point of view. But no system has ever been suggested for objectively identifying such points along the continuum, nor has anyone ever tackled the fundamental problem of where the centre is. Neither have any criteria ever been adduced for defining titles along this continuum, nor for even confirming the existence of a continuum. How, indeed, would one arrange the array of items in the listings at the end of this book? Is sexual politics more left than anarchism? Is environmental activism more centre than human rights research? Are they all at the extreme left of the continuum? If so, do counterbalancing items exist? The adversarial British political system tends to encourage the division of issues into left, right and centre, yet such a division is not tenable as a classification scheme of knowledge and information.

It may make no sense to talk of a 'balanced collection', but it is surely meaningful to consider providing information and knowledge on topics from as wide an array as possible. Let us do away with notions of left, right and centre and consider how adding certain titles to our libraries can enhance material already there and thereby improve the users' access to viewpoints enormously. Incorporating alternative literature into our collections is part of such a project.

The invisibility of alternative literature in the market place

Whilst the alternative press will comment at great length and in great depth on mainstream culture and media, the reverse is rarely true. (It then follows that the alternative literature will be the best place to find out about the alternative literature.) *The London Review of Books* may well have reviewed Seumas Milne's *The enemy within* (Verso) and the *Times Literary Supplement* tends to review the political writings of Noam Chomsky published by Pluto Press and Verso, but this is as far along the alternative road as the mainstream media normally go. We should not be surprised at this, nor should we cry conspiracy. Inevitably there will be an element of snobbery about what passes for literature in such circles. Paperback titles without spines and with obviously photocopied copies will arouse the contempt or, at best, distrust of the mainstream reviewer. But even those titles that accord with the professional standards of mainstream book publishing tend to fair poorly (and this regardless of content). Most alternative titles are simply beyond the purview of mainstream reviewers. This is largely to do with the constraints that operate on the editors and publishers of such review journals. It is obvious enough that items will only be considered for review if they are brought to the attention of such people. Alternative publishers operating on shoestring budgets, not for profit, can ill afford to send out too many review copies. They know that the chance of getting a review in a mainstream journal is virtually nil, so they will tend to distribute review copies amongst the alternative press itself, where they will find a more sympathetic audience.

Since the enormous selectivity that takes place in all main-stream review pages precludes even the majority of mainstream titles from garnering reviews, what chance have the thousands of obscure, small circulation alternative titles got? This applies equally to the dedicated review journals such as *The London Review of Books* and the *Times Literary Supplement* as well as to specialist subject journals. As circulation increases, so does selectivity, reaching its apogee in the daily papers, where a mere handful of titles – all firmly mainstream – are considered each week.

The advertising budget of any large publisher will typically exceed that of a small press by a hundredfold (at least). Mailshots, newspaper and magazine advertising, television and radio coverage: all will ensure that both librarians and library users will encounter mainstream publications (whatever the subject) as part of their daily life. The review pages of the broadsheet newspapers choose the majority of their titles from the mainstream; displays of 'books reviewed' are increasingly common in bookstores and libraries.

But there is more to this than financial constraints. The attitude within the book trade – although changing a little – is far from equanimous. Titles may be treated with suspicion, if not with downright ridicule for not being 'proper books' from 'proper publishers'. The stocking of alternative titles by mainstream distributors, bookstores and library suppliers is at best patchy, often non-existent (save for the few established 'major' alternatives). In this respect alone alternative titles may be viewed as a type of grey literature. They certainly exhibit similar characteristics that account for their poor treatment by the book trade at large:

1. Low profit margins.
2. 'Non-professional' layout and design.
3. Unknown authors and/or novel subject matter.

Low profit margins

Much alternative publishing is perforce done on a low budget.

The ethic behind much of it is non-profit making: titles produced by Freedom Press of London, for instance, retail for as much as 50 per cent less than a mainstream title of similar extent (in both size and coverage) – indeed, so cheap are their titles that they have had to prevent another not-for-profit organization from distributing their titles at wholesale prices to individual customers, since the losses incurred by such a practice are too high. The cut to a wholesaler, distributor or bookstores can be so low that many in the trade consider such purchases as little more than an act of charity, rather than a commercial undertaking.

'Non-professional' layout and design

Many titles do not get as far as bookshops simply because they are not spined or do not meet other standards of presentation such as colour covers or professional printing. As in mainstream publishing, alternative publishing uses all the available media for its publications. There are, however, a number of formats and types of publications that only exist within alternative publishing. The ubiquity of the photocopier as a publishing tool means that book and periodical sizes conform to A and B sizes more than they do to traditional book sizes. The folded-to-A5, stapled publication will be found as a book, a periodical and a pamphlet in alternative publications. Only the number of pages might distinguish one from the other. Whilst we will find hundreds of titles whose production standards are indistinguishable from those of the mainstream, non-standard sizes such as A6 and A7 are remarkably common amongst small presses. (Playtime Forever Press has reprinted all its 'Penny Dreadful' A4 pamphlets as A7 booklets.) These are considered problematic, since they are deemed unsuitable for shelving amongst 'standard size' stock, although one might see such items in 'non-retail' outlets such as record and comic shops. Such locations are often more sympathetic to their style and content, since they accord well with their existing stock and customers' expectations. The high street bookshop will often – for precisely the same reasons, the integrity of the stock and the perceived desires of its customers – choose to reject such stock.

Unknown authors and/or novel subject matter

No commercial interest enjoys taking risks, certainly not many at a time. The risks of taking titles by unknown authors or on novel subjects will be minimized by the backing of a substantial marketing budget or the guaranteed widespread publicity that accrues to a Lyall Watson or an Erik von Daniken, say. Rare indeed is the mainstream bookshop that stocks alternative titles in any number, but Ramsey Kanaan of AK Press and Distribution has found that bookshops will often be tempted by the unknown once the allure of more mainstream alternative titles has been successfully proved: 'Everyone wants *Society of the Spectacle*, everyone wants Chomsky ... If we say we've got Chomsky and Guy Debord and some Autonomedia, Baudrillard and Foucault, they're gonna go crazy [for them]. And then we say, we've also got this stuff. And then they usually take it on the back of the stuff that they want.'[13] Many bookstores will still tell you – and their advertising of this is becoming increasingly prominent since the advent of online ordering systems – that they can and will order for you any book they have in stock. But for many people this is analogous to the present situation in the chain record shops: there's no vinyl, but they will order it for you. A supermarket run on such lines would go out of business tomorrow, founded as it is on choice at the shelf, not via mail order. But there is a belief that such a service is actually a boon to customers rather than a barrier. Yet where will the customer discover that such a title exists, in order to be able to order it? As Jon Carpenter of Jon Carpenter Publishing has noted: 'Bookshops only really serve a useful purpose if they stock books. They are a very inefficient (and inflationary) way of handling single customer orders.'[14]

Library suppliers

Approvals collections from suppliers can only include what the supplier has already chosen and bought, a choice based on what they believe can be sold on to the librarian. Do library suppliers buy alternative publications as a matter of course? The views of two major UK library suppliers are about as robust a pair of views that we will find. Firstly, Duncan Turner of James Askew & Son believes it is the 'sales and marketing failures' which prevent alternative titles from being identified and acquired by library suppliers. He is confident, however, that such failures represent only 'a few titles by obscure experimental publishers'.[15] The sales and marketing manager of Greenhead Books, Nigel Lancaster, does not go so far as to claim that his company are aware of the majority of titles published in the UK, but he has said that Greenhead are 'willing and able to supply any available publication, whatever the source'.[16] Two views, two issues: factually, Duncan Turner must be wrong. Askew just don't stock that much – no library supplier does, not even the specialist distributors. He misreads the publishing situation in the UK drastically, if he believes there are 'only a few' that are missed by him or any other library supplier. Nigel Lancaster's assertion raises the question of availability linked with accessibility: how do you know a title exists? Even if you do, how do you know where to get it from? Where do you get *The Bug* from? Where do you get *Fatuous Times* from? This should not be taken as a criticism of any particular library supplier; it is simply in the nature of their work that they do not tend to hold exhaustive collections of alternative literature. Rather it is the great claims made by suppliers that we should be sceptical about.

There simply is little standardization or control over bibliographic information in this field, and what control exists is wholly inadequate for a mainstream supplier to supply anything like an exhaustive ordering service. We must either help them by providing far more information than we are accustomed to doing for mainstream items or we must deal directly with a multiplicity of specialist distributors and the publishers themselves. We must also start taking risks, trusting the purveyors: 'We urge you to try out some of the unknown or unfamiliar material we handle', plead Counter Productions in their catalogue. They are right, of course: for it is only by purchasers taking risks that marginal work will flourish – or at any event, circulate.

The problems of bibliographic control

The underground press of the late 1960s and early 1970s was effectively destroyed by the establishment employing spurious accusations of obscenity and drug connections to frighten and prosecute writers and publishers into oblivion. The small number of publications – no more than a few hundred, each with a relatively large circulation – made intimidation more effective. Suspects were identifiable; the network was finite; the geography of the underground could be accurately mapped. As they were re-reading Geoffrey Rips's account of these events,[17] the editors of *Bypass* were struck by the impossibility of such a task today, when there are thousands of publications, most with very small circulations – circulations that fluctuate, are temporary, often untraceable. 'Decentralization not only gives people a voice ... It may prove a key strategy for the survival of dissent, or even just plain old independent thinking in a society that seems to be getting more and more authoritarian every year.'[18]

But what might be of benefit to protest movements and the authors of alternative literature is a positive disadvantage to anyone attempting to make sense of the bewildering range and the exponential expansion of alternative literature. Titles that have ISBNs and ISSNs will of course show up in mainstream bibliographic tools such as *Global Books in Print* and *Ulrich's* (as one of the few free methods of gaining visibility in the mainstream commercial world of publishing and bookselling), but this will account for only a small proportion of alternative publications. Although more and more publishers make use of the numbering systems and cataloguing-in-publication data (notwithstanding its faults), they tend to be ones that operate their distribution on more-or-less mainstream lines. Other take an avowedly ideological stance against such systems of control. Fred Woodworth, editor of *The Match!*, a long-running anarchist journal, has announced that he will no longer print reviews of books that have ISBNs, since he considers the ISBN as a state licence for books. There are still others who are quite unaware of such things, and who would not be much interested in them were you to tell them.

Utilizing standard, mainstream bibliographic sources will not only provide an extremely limited range of alternative literature, they will also prevent any understanding or appreciation of the literature. These are essential undertakings if we are to properly integrate such titles into our work. There are a handful of alternative bibliographic sources that resemble mainstream publications, but we will also find a variety of non-traditional, unique publications that are nevertheless of immense value in identifying, understanding and acquiring material across the whole range of alternative literature.

Faced with a range of publications whose growth appears out of control; growth which cannot be monitored due to the lack of centralized bibliographic control; publications that can disappear almost as quickly as they have appeared, due to short print runs; publications that are largely unavailable through mainstream bookshops and library suppliers; publications that hardly have a presence in other libraries – even in our national libraries – making inter-library lending very difficult: how can the librarian or researcher be confident that all sources of information have been examined; that all titles have been identified; that all have been adequately assessed for research or purchase? How can they be sure that whatever methods they use will prove reliable or successful next time?

These questions are exacerbated when we consider that with alternative literature the librarian or researcher is not simply trying to identify documents in the way one might with *Global Books in Print* or the *British National Bibliography*. Since discussion of alternative literature is almost completely absent from mainstream literature, we also need to get inside it, so to speak. The workings of the mainstream publishing and distribution industries become known to us as a matter of course during our professional education, or simply by working with them. The general contours of their publications, how they come to be written and even the kinds of people who become authors are also known to us.

Our knowledge of these areas may not be exhaustive – it may not even be accurate – but it suffices to enable us to make confident and (apparently) well-informed decisions about selecting and evaluating. We come to recognize and trust – even rely upon – certain authors, publishers and distributors as reliable sources of information. However much we might consider ourselves immune from the predations of advertising, still we shall be tempted by the recommendations of reviewers and blurb writers we know, especially when we recognize them as authors of books we have already acquired. We have already seen how the minimal advertising budget of alternative publishers ensures that we will not learn about their titles through our usual methods of selection. When one sets out to undertake mainstream bibliographic searching, evaluation and selection for the first time, one may find it time-consuming and exhausting. It may also appear of dubious value, for one's ignorance of the 'wider picture' of mainstream publishing makes it unlikely that we will have covered even one topic adequately. As our experience increases, so does our expertise and our confidence. We discover short cuts, some of which will be of positive value, saving us time as well as getting us to the information we want. Some of them, though, will surely restrict our searching. We will come to rely on specific suppliers, place our trust in those publishers we know, give priority to authors whose works we already have.

Our forays into alternative literature might well easily follow a similar line. The only difference is that even were we to reach the short cuts, say by selecting from a narrow range of alternative publishers and distributors, we will still be selecting from a much wider range, as a whole, than we were when we stayed within the confines of the mainstream. But starting along that road can appear fraught with difficulty. For many it must seem as if they must learn new techniques of bibliographic searching, of evaluation and selection. Their knowledge of mainstream publishing, whilst not to be discarded, might seem of little use. Recognizing and relying on familiar names and subjects, even relying on particular forms of expression, all will be of little help. But if we are persuaded of the value of alternative literature both as a counter to prevailing ideas and perspectives and as a fund of new ideas and perspectives, then we need to begin along that road. What follows is intended to guide anyone considering such a journey, although it cannot hope to be an exhaustive guide to all points on that journey. There are many crossroads, detours and cul-de-sacs in alternative literature, but these are best ignored for the present, whilst we concentrate on the more straightforward path.

References

1. Department of National Heritage's *Review of the Public Library Service in England and Wales: Draft Report September 1994*, prepared by Aslib Consultancy (London: Aslib,1994).
2. Buhle Mbambo, 'Censorship in Southern Africa: how does it affect collection development?' (unpublished manuscript).
3. 'The friendless pagan recluse', *The Guardian*, 15 September 1994, p. 5.
4. Ian Malley, *Censorship and Libraries* (London: Library Association, 1990), p. 30.
5. Alan M. Linfield, 'A sorry tale of missing books' (letter), *Library Association Record* **92**(9), September 1990, p. 650.
6. Documented by John Gray in 'Censorship and the current Northern Ireland Bibliography', *Linen Hall Review* **4**(1), Spring 1987, pp. 6–8.
7. Ian Malley, *Censorship and Libraries*, p. 30.
8. Documented by Alison Behr, 'LA issues gay rights guide ...' and '... as Section 28 saga continues', *Library Association Record* **97**(3), March 1995, p.140.
9. Anthony Hugh Thompson, *Censorship in public libraries in the United Kingdom during the twentieth century* (Epping: Bowker, 1975), pp. 56–7 and p. 127.
10. 'Extremists make use of Internet' and 'Anarchism runs riot on the superhighway', *Computing*, 2 March 1995, p.1 and p. 6. Adrian Levy and Ian Burrell, 'Anarchists use computers to spread terror', *Sunday Times* (Scottish Edition), 5 March 1995, p. 10.
11. Noam Chomksy, *Keeping the rabble in line: interviews with David Barsamian* (Edinburgh: AK Press, 1994), p.153.
12. 'Objectivity and Bias' (editorial), *EIF News*, (2), January 1995, p. 1.

13. 'Distribution in a capitalist world: AK Distribution on the move: an interview with Ramsey Kanaan', *Alternative Press Review* (2), Winter 1994, pp. 10-16.

14. Letter to customers, September 1994.

15. Duncan Turner, 'Stock selection: the library supplier's view', *Scottish Libraries*, May/June 1993, pp. 10-11.

16. Nigel Lancaster, 'Regular review please' (letter), *Assistant Librarian*, August 1992, p.121.

17. Geoffrey Rips, *The campaign against the underground press* (London: City Limits, 1981).

18. Untitled editorial, *Bypass* (3), 1994, unpaginated.

5 Acquiring Alternative Literature

A strategy for identifying alternative publications

We should not expect to be able to know all titles in all subjects, nor should we expect some simple overview; after all, can we envisage having such knowledge or obtaining such an overview for mainstream literature? There are alternative equivalents to the likes of *Global Books in Print* and *British National Bibliography*, for those needing the most exhaustive listing, but there is no guidebook to alternative literature as a whole, just as there is no guide to mainstream literature as a whole.

Let us start by getting a feel – no more than that – for what alternative literature and its publishing and distribution operations are about. The best place for this is in the alternative press itself. *Alternative Press Review* is a quarterly that reprints articles from the whole range of the alternative press, from the political magazines to the personal zines. It also acts as an 'industry spotlight', running interviews and in-depth features on specialist publishers and subject areas. In its back pages will be found a few dozen magazine reviews and one or two featured book reviews. For its reprinted articles and industry features alone it is invaluable for providing an overview of the nature of alternative publishing, both its contents and its techniques. But for many people, including Bill and Linda Sternberg Katz, who call it 'the single most important magazine for librarians interested in current alternative periodical literature',[1] *Utne Reader* is considered the cream of the alternative press reviews. Yet it has been continually moving towards the more mainstream alternative media such as *Village Voice*, and even reprinting from *The Wall Street Journal*. Although it does not boast the 150 pages of its glossy competitor, *Alternative Press Review* presents reprints that are far more representative of what the alternative press says and does. The picture one would get from only reading *Utne Reader* would be skewed indeed. *New pages: alternatives in print & media*, *Small Press* and *Small Press News* provide news and developments and some reviews of publications within the alternative publishing trade. Be aware that these mostly examine literary publishing or the more established independent presses producing more mainstream material. You will find only some discussion of current affairs, anarchism and similar 'alternative' topics. The Radical Booksellers' Network of the US publishes a newsletter *Fire in the mind* which, although aimed at alternative bookshops, contains some useful columns for librarians, including personal top tens of alternative titles, lists of recently remaindered titles and a 'books received' list. (It is a matter for regret that the UK's Radical Bookseller network cased to exist in 1992, along with its journal *Radical Bookseller* and the important *Radical Bookseller Directory*.)

U-Direct grew out of the first Underground Press Conference, held in Chicago in 1994. *U-Direct* contains extensive features, columns and personal views on all aspects of alternative publishing from the publishers themselves, and is as valuable and as painless an introduction to what they are doing as you will find anywhere. There is no British equivalent to any of these titles. *Bypass* is the closest we have which, although primarily a review journal for books, journals and zines, does include brief extracts from publications, as well as brief but informative features on copyright, freedom of information and distribution networks.

Fortunately the international outlook of many small publishers, and the priority they give to networking and the sharing of information ensures that the publications in this chapter consider the UK in their articles and listings.

There are few books to help us find our way through the literature. The majority of published accounts of the alternative press are historical, focusing on the 1960s and 1970s, the 'underground' press. Even those titles published expressly for the librarian, such as Mick Hoey's little *The alternative press in Britain: a select bibliography* (Brighton: Smoothie, 1973) are now useless as introductions to contemporary alternative literature. The only contemporary account that is at all comprehensive and meaningful is Bob Black's *Beneath the underground,* a collection of reviews and essays on what he calls 'the marginals milieu'. Black writes from one of the most informed perspectives possible (he was in at the beginning of the latest wave of alternative publishing in the late 1970s). His accounts of the Situationists (his little bibliography here nicely reduces their output to a few pages of well-chosen titles), The Church of the SubGenius, *Factsheet 5,* the Loompanics Unlimited catalogue and many other alternatives are not simply accounts of contemporary publishing interventions, they are examples of these in their own right.

Apart from the present text, *Alternative materials in libraries,* edited by James P. Danky and Elliott Shore, remains the only handbook aimed at librarians. It contains chapters on developing appropriate cataloguing practices for alternative materials and on identifying abstracts and indexes and other reference tools. Technical and reference information is supplemented by personal essays from alternative publishers about their dealings with libraries, along with more rigorous examinations of the status of alternative materials in libraries. Finally there is a directory of all the alternative sources cited, along with separate directories of suppliers of non-print materials and of established collections of contemporary alternative materials. Despite its age (and the corresponding out-of-dateness of some of its sources), this remains a central work for any librarian or researcher. A new edition would be invaluable.

Danky is also the co-editor (with Sanford Berman) of

Alternative library literature: a biennial anthology. Begun in 1982, this series might be thought of as an updating service to the previous book. Each volume reprints articles taken from the mainstream and the alternative periodical press, including mainstream and alternative library presses. A magazine directory at the end of each volume provides addresses and prices, whilst a typically exhaustive index by Sanford Berman ensures that the whole text is extremely accessible.

The reprints are gathered under sections, one of which ('Alternatives') deals explicitly with sources of alternative publications (publishers and publications, selection and acquisition). A number of bibliographies and reading lists appear in each volume, and other sections deal with social responsibility issues such as censorship, peace, empowerment, services to minority groups and the role of the librarian in society.

Many of the journals excerpted in *Alternative Library Literature*, whilst not alternative literature themselves, often include articles of interest to anyone researching or selecting in this field. Journals such as *Collection Building*, *Multicultural Review* and *Serials Review* have published many articles and bibliographies that include alternative materials. Robert M. Gorman's 'Selecting new right materials – a case study' (*Collection Building* 8(3) 1987, 3–8) and Chris Dodge's 'Alternative sex: some 'zines, comics, books, and sources' (*Collection Building* 13(1) 1993, 48–51) are two such examples (the latter featured as part of a regular 'Alternatives' column, edited by Sanford Berman).

Bibliographic tools for acquisitions

The phrase 'bibliographic tool' is of course a librarian's naming device. Only a few of the titles that follow would be thought of as 'bibliographic tools' by their editors and publishers. Many are in fact directed at the individual purchaser and are in fact simply descriptive mail-order catalogues. Yet in the world of alternative literature we must be prepared to take advantage of whatever sources come our way. To grace them with the nomenclature of library science, whilst somewhat inaccurate, will at least remind us of the purpose they serve and alert us to future publications that similarly might not resemble the accustomed tools of our trade, but which still may prove indispensable.

What follows is a listing of the most comprehensive bibliographic tools currently available. They concentrate on titles that are general in their outlook and present the librarian and researcher with a range of titles, publishers and distributors. It is through such titles as these that the more specialist sources – such as those described in Chapters 2 and 3 – may be located. At this stage, though, it is more appropriate to identify titles that not only demonstrate the immense coverage of alternative literature but at the same time offer context and some measure of description of the items they list.

Bibliographies

APT for Libraries [date]: Alternative Press Titles for the General Reader
Surely the selection tool of greatest single value to librarians seeking to acquire alternative literature, since it is produced by a (former) acquisitions librarian for librarians. Its strengths lie in the wide range of subjects covered, its currency and its admitted aim to provide titles 'for the general reader'. It covers every area of alternative publishing in all forms: journal, zine, pamphlet, book, electronic. Its subject coverage includes all topics that characterize the alternative publishing scene: multicultural issues; gay and lesbian; media critiques; economics; environmental issues; peace studies; human rights; censorship; women's studies; international affairs. It is published annually, its contents a distillation of the featured titles of the previous alternative press exhibitions held by CRISES Press at the two previous ALA national conferences.

It does have its shortcomings, however, and these are readily admitted by its publisher. Since the catalogues are based on exhibitors' titles on a trade stand, only publishers who can afford to exhibit there will get their work listed in the catalogues (even though the charges are on a sliding scale). The economics of production dictate that *APT for Libraries* is by necessity an edited list of the two catalogues, so the selection process is further limited (the catalogues themselves are also available from CRISES Press).

CultureWatch: a monthly annotated bibliography on culture, art and political affairs
Founded in 1993, each four-page issue contains some 40 reviews of current articles and new books on political, social and economic issues, drawn from over 500 periodicals and reports. Its aim, in Charles Willett's words, is 'to document the rise of the Right in the politics of culture in America'.[2] In addition to the reviews, it also provides information on publications, organizations and campaigns that are struggling against encroaching conservatism in public and private life. Another no-profit centre working for social justice and social change, the Datacenter's library contains clipping files on 'all public policy issues drawn from over 400 periodicals'.

Review journals

The sanctioned mainstream review journals for libraries in the US are *Choice* and *Booklist*. In the UK there is only *The Bookseller*. These dominate in the purchasing and acquisition of titles. But their treatment of the alternative press and of alternative perspectives on mainstream subjects is far from equal to their treatment of the products of the major publishing houses. Charles Willett has noted the in-built biases of reviewers in *Choice* magazine against 'politically controversial monographs' and demanded that ' Review journals should put aside ideology and guarantee that all viewpoints on controversial or sensitive topics are fairly evaluated'.[3] *The Bookseller* fares better, and has featured the larger alternative presses when examining, for instance, gay and lesbian publishing. Yet it still ignores the majority of alternative titles published in the UK. Redressing the balance are a number of review journals that concentrate exclusively on alternative titles. Most are of US origin, but without exception they feature material from the UK, Ireland and Canada in their pages.

Bypass
Since the demise of *News from Neasden* in the early 1980s and the (temporary?) disappearance of *Small Press World*, this is the only British alternative review journal, indeed, the only regular general source of information about alternative publishing in the UK. We have already encountered it when discussing zines, but it also provides many book and pamphlet reviews of the smaller alternative presses (in other words, most of them) being the only source of reviews in Britain for most of what it covers. It also runs features on specific publishers and distributors and has run articles on information sources on the peace movement in the former Yugoslavia and the British phenomenon of Free Information Networks.

Counterpoise
Due to be launched in 1996 under the auspices of the American Library Association, through the Alternatives in Print Task Force of its Social Responsibilities Round Table. *Counterpoise* should provide a comprehensive alternative to the ALA's long-standing titles *Booklist* and *Choice* and will be the only dedicated review journal for alternative literature produced explicitly by librarians for librarians. It aims to review alternative materials in the English language in all formats (books, zines, pamphlets, audiovisual, computer databases and software) and will therefore look further than simply the US for its reviews, including Canada, the UK, Ireland, the anglophone countries of Africa and beyond in its remit. Details on its progress are available from the Alternatives in Print Task Force Co-ordinator, Charles Willett, at the CRISES Press address and in the UK from Information for Social Change, which will be coordinating the British input.

Factsheet 5
Like *Bypass*, this has already been mentioned when discussing zines. Its coverage of books, records and videos is increasing all

the time, and although it does not achieve the (numerical) balance between these resources that *Bypass* does, it should not only be considered just for information about zines.

MSRRT Newsletter (Newsletter of the Minnesota Library Association's Social Responsibilities Round Table)
Although expressly produced for a local group of librarians, this is the only review journal of alternative literature for libraries, covering publications from the US, UK and Canada. Each issue opens with news and comment on social responsibility issues within librarianship and in wider contexts. This is followed by a couple of pages of recommended books and reference works. The bulk of the newsletter is taken up with reviews of periodicals received. Each issue features around 30 zines, newsletters and journals, supplemented by notices of changes of journal title and organizational names, and books and catalogues received. The subject range and latest titles in each catalogue is briefly described. Its updating column of periodical title and address changes is of great value. For those looking for a manageable, approachable guide to alternative literature of all types and topics, featuring information and criticism this is an excellent place to start.

Sipapu
The second oldest small press review journal in the US (the oldest being *Small Press Review*), founded in 1969. Largely written by the editor (Noel Peattie, a former librarian at the University of California, Davis and long-time champion of the small press), *Sipapu* is aimed directly at librarians (and 'collectors'). It is written in continuous prose, Peattie's fluid, relaxing style moving the reader easily from one title to the next. It's a little like reading an account of whatever is on Peattie's desk at the time, sprinkled with some pertinent conversation on matters of social responsibility and censorship. Access to the titles reviewed is by way of a multi-sectioned index of books, journals and obituaries. An inspired work, well-sustained and friendly, informative and informed. (Unfortunately its editor

announced the cessation of *Sipapu* from the end of 1995, although back issues are still available.)

Small Press Book Review
Deals with the 'independent' publishers, that is, the larger, better-established alternative publishers. Consequently their subject matter is more mainstream than most of that covered in this book. It is currently being published electronically and although at present not prepared to handle foreign subscriptions, the publisher may e-mail it to those interested in it overseas.

Small Press Review (incorporating *Small Magazine Review*)
Edited by Len Fulton at Dustbooks, this doubles as a monthly update to his *Directory of little magazines and small presses* between its annual appearance, providing names, addresses and descriptions of new titles and publishers as they become known to him. It is also the most frequent review journal we have for the output of such publishers, and although the emphasis is – as the nomenclature 'small press' suggests – firmly on poetry and fiction, titles of social and political interest do appear.

Sourcebooks

Included here are both distributors' catalogues and books that draw from the titles of a range of publishers and aim to introduce their readers to the subjects they cover. Although the latter are not written by distributors, they can be thought of as a cross between a collection of reviews and a distributor's catalogue. The inclusion of distributors' catalogues might appear facile; they are after all hardly unique to alternative literature, nor are they generally considered to be special bibliographic tools. Yet there are a few that, whilst not claiming to be comprehensive, are still useful starting points for anyone investigating alternative literature from scratch. This is especially true of those that usefully combine explanatory text, illustrations, addresses and ordering information. Beyond their use as a simple acquisitions tool they can help us appreciate the range of information available in a particular subject and provide an overview of that subject. Many publishers realize that – unlike their mainstream counterparts – most of their titles will be unfamiliar to the readers of their catalogues, and so they will often provide basic introductions (and sometimes detailed explanations and extracts of their titles) to the subject matter. They understand that their customers are unlikely to take risks without first having at least an inkling of what the titles contain. Finally they will also provide some indication of the current state of the alternative press at any particular time.

Given that alternative publishing is always in flux, many of the items listed in these titles here will become unavailable quickly. This will not negate the value of these books entirely, however, since they will all contain enough that remains current and provide a reliable enough flavour of the breadth and nature of alternative publishing.

Covert culture sourcebook and *Covert culture sourcebook 2.0* by Richard Kadrey
As the author admits, he has 'no intention of putting things in perspective for you ... no interest in telling you what to think'. His and his reviewers' selections in both volumes is partial, but then he makes no claims to completeness. What he presents here is an overview of some of the dominant themes in alternative culture (his 'covert culture') described in terms of the publications and other products available. Not all the items here are the products of alternative publishing: many of the recordings listed, for instance, are on mainstream labels. Rather it is their content that is highlighted here. Each item is briefly reviewed and many are accompanied with a reproduction of the cover. Ordering information and addresses are added to each title (though there are a few omissions). They are arranged by format: Books, Zines, Music, Video and Tools for Living (this last a miscellany including CD-ROM, fashion and 'sex tools'). The second volume replaces the section on zines with sections on comics, electronic zines and the Internet. All other sections contain entirely new selections. Each format is subdivided by subject. Unfortunately the indexes effectively repeat this arrangement,

resulting in a format–subject–title hierarchy that is useless as an index. Consequently it is not possible to make detailed subject searches across formats. Since all items are recommendations, the style is upbeat, often uncritical and superficial. Kadrey admits that anyone could compile such a book themselves and could well do it better than he. (The fact remains that to date no one else has.) But as one partial window on alternative publishing across all formats, these volumes provide a well-illustrated, simple and wide-ranging introduction to the kinds of titles available. Kadrey also offers free quarterly updates on the publishers and organizations reviewed, 'including some new reviews'.

The Millenium Whole Earth Catalog: access to tools and ideas for the twenty-first century, Howard Rheingold, ed.
This is the third edition of the *Whole Earth Catalog*, which has appeared roughly every decade since 1971, now with a mainstream publisher (yet its importance ensures it a place here, virtually the only mainstream title in this book). This latest edition is very much of its time: taking note that the environmental and ecological interventions it has championed previously now have a momentum of their own, it has cast its net wider. Arranged into 14 broad categories, it encompasses such topics as local political empowerment, independent education, health and 'taming technology', in addition to the typical *Whole Earth Review* areas like biodiversity and sustainability. Its exuberant style and large format make it an extremely readable volume. It covers a large range of organizations, books, pamphlets, journals, electronic sources and household and leisure goods, providing a brief description of each and frequent selections from the publications cited. At its heart is individual empowerment and the promotion of social change through raising people's awareness of the range of information available. At times it reads a little like a consumer magazine for the socially responsible and its page layouts resemble mail-order catalogues for household goods. It does boast a decent index, however, that lists all items and subjects covered. Essentially it is a selection of the best of the quarterly *Whole Earth Review*, which should be consulted for updates and additions.

Distributors' catalogues

AK Press and Distribution, Counter Productions and Turnaround Distribution together represent the bulk of titles and publishers distributed in the UK. Between them they cover an impressively wide range, from extremely limited editions and small circulation pamphlets, through anarchist and other independent political writings, to alternative fiction, poetry and all matters cultural. AK and Counter Productions are the prime sources for alternative periodicals. So paradigmatic of the depth and diversity of alternative publishing is the stock carried by AK Press and Distribution and Counter Productions that their catalogues are considered in some detail in two 'case studies' at the end of this section. Turnaround Distribution is especially strong on gay and lesbian publishing, both fiction and non-fiction. Indeed it publishes a gay and lesbian catalogue equal in size to its 'main catalogue' which features a wide range of fiction publishers as well as a handful of the smaller presses also distributed by AK and Counter (AK Press itself, Attack International, Feral House, Phoenix Press).

Along with Jon Carpenter, Turnaround Distribution also handles the long-standing publishers of social change literature such as South End Press (Turnaround), Black Rose Books (Jon Carpenter and Turnaround) and New Society (Jon Carpenter).

Left Bank Distribution covers similar ground to AK and declares itself,'the largest provider of anarchist and independent radical books in North America', handling over 1 200 titles from over 100 publishers. It also runs its own publishing house, a used books service (AKA Books) and a bookshop, Left Bank Books. Its catalogue comprises a single alphabetical sequence by title, with an author index and brief descriptions and recommendations throughout.

The catalogues of Amok and Loompanics Unlimited inhabit the more extreme end of alternative publishing. Indeed, Amok's catalogue is subtitled 'Sourcebook of the Extremes of Information in Print' and a book in its own right, being a large format catalogue covering topics that are nevertheless at the heart of much alternative publishing, profusely illustrated and containing many excerpts from the titles it distributes. Whilst far from the last word on the topics it covers (the fourth edition, whilst still current, is now four years old) can still function as an introductory, desk reference to the genres and fields it covers, such as sex and sexuality, media and censorship, extremes of politics, parapolitics and conspiracy, fringe science, and body art. It has been accused by at least one commentator (Michael Ventura) of 'profiting from the predatory' (this remark is reproduced without comment in the catalogue itself). The attitude of Amok and Loompanics Unlimited to the material is perhaps best summarized by the coordinator of a similar service, Gary Franklin of The Centre for the Academic Study of Extremes in Human Experience Research Project, as 'dedicated to the research and understanding of all of the wide varieties of abnormal experiences and deviance that humans are subject to and/or are subjected to within a humanistic and sociological context'. Loompanics Unlimited take this approach even further, stating that they 'don't care about anything except having fun and your right to find out anything you want to know'. They deal in what might be loosely called 'forbidden knowledge'. This includes titles on censorship and the mass media, self-defence and survivalism, cooking with unusual ingredients (especially animals), government reports on the use of assassination and torture to achieve political ends, drugs, dropping out, how to conduct your own investigations and self-publishing. It is certainly the largest and most unusual collection of alternative 'how to' books ever found in one catalogue. (Some of the advice and activities contained in some of their titles would be illegal if carried out. Loompanics Unlimited are therefore careful to declare that 'all titles are sold for informational purposes only'.)

For assessing the range of zines and periodicals available, we have already noted *Bypass* and *Factsheet 5* as the key sources here, but we should also consider the well-illustrated catalogues of the two major alternative periodical distributors Fine Print and Desert Moon Periodicals/Xines, Inc. Both are arranged by subject and make valuable reference works as well as ordering tools.

Distributor case study 1: AK Distribution

AK Press describes itself as publishing 'everything from poetry to parapolitics and most in between', a description that also serves to describe its distribution arm, specializing in thousands of small press and individually published titles covering anarchist, libertarian and situationist material, in addition to much poetry and prose. Its most well-known authors include Noam Chomsky, Tom Leonard, Murray Bookchin and James Kelman. But AK's strength lies in the equal space it gives to the unknown, the anonymous and the collective authors of titles that offer insights into the cultural and political life of our country (and indeed, of the world). Tracts and polemics such as Gerry Mander's *Four Arguments for the Elimination of Television, Dear Motorist ... the social ideology of the motor car*, and Robert Lynn's *Vote: what for?* Alternatives to our increasingly ideologically-determined educational system might also be found: John Shotton's history of libertarian education in Britain, *No master high or low*, is a book rare amongst mainstream publications: an educational work that has no pretensions to academia, that can be as easily and as profitably read by parents and children as by academics.

Nowhere is the élitist argument better put to flight than in AK's poetry, prose and comic collections. Tom Leonard, Benjamin Zephaniah and Henry Normal sit alongside the violent fiction of Stewart Home (described by one mainstream critic as having 'no literary merit') and *End Time*, the apocalyptic first novel by G. A. Matiasz. Leo Baxendale, Robert Crumb and Clifford Harper are some of the better-known names that populate the comics corner.

As a major distributor of alternative journals and magazines AK is able to offer the investigative journalism and parapolitics of *CovertAction Quarterly* and *Lobster*, the environmental activism of *Earth First! Journal* and *Green Anarchist*, the uncategorizable *Casablanca* and *The Bug*. This is to leave aside what are almost veterans of the alternative press scene: *Anarchy, Black Flag, Troops Out*, and *Z Magazine*. And on and on: for every left, communist, anarchist and libertarian political persuasion; for every single-issue cause; for every area of concern and research there is a journal, be it glossy, photocopied, perfect bound, stapled, loose-leaf; weekly, quarterly, or (the serial librarian's nightmare) the wilfully irregular. AK is an excellent source for all of these.

Distributor case study 2: Counter Productions

Less explicitly 'political' than AK, yet its stocklist must rank as one of the most enlightening and curious of the small press distributors: it claims as its own such areas as 'dissident, surreal, outré, pataphysical and anti-authoritarian'. The recommendations in its catalogue impress with a degree of honesty that is rare in the world of publishing. Counter Productions are often fiercely independent from the stock they are selling and will tell you honestly if they are disappointed with a title they stock – labelling it 'for real fans only' or 'if you're new to this , get x instead'. A favourite is 'overpriced – worth ordering from the library, but don't buy it yourself'. They are willing to share both their mistakes and their successes with their customers: 'The plea on which this operation is founded: try something unknown, surprise yourself.'

At first glance the Counter Productions catalogue seems to be thrown together with no logic at all. Infuriating, but an affirmation of the fluidity of much of the material that Counter Productions handle. Their titles defy all but the most outré or otiose of categories. Their very immunity to easy categorization means that they sit uneasily even amongst the subjects already examined in previous chapters. Counter Productions needs a category all its own. Its internal logic might be quite opaque, but its stocklist is unique.

The catalogue begins with the reprint series of Aporia Press, introducing a modern audience to the English revolutionary writings of the Ranters and the Diggers; Gerard Winstanley and Abiezer Coppe. These are followed by the classic surrealist works of André Breton, Raymond Queneau and Benjamin Peret, published by such as Atlas Press. The heirs of such writers include authors of 'enthused writings' like Harry Mathews and Jacques Roubaud, published by Dalkey Archive Press. Malice Aforethought Press and Indelible Inc. publish some of the most accessible English fiction by such as Ellis Sharp and Frank Key.

The unclassifiable eccentricities of Mark Pawson's tiny, self-produced booklets take the DIY publishing ethic to new heights: *Mark's Little Book About Kinder Eggs* meticulously documents the most noteworthy of his collection of over 500 Kinder Egg toys, all fully illustrated, described and evaluated; *Eco-Frenzy* reproduces dozens of recycling symbols from product packaging and street furniture.

The anomalous phenomena of Fortean investigations are well covered by Counter Productions. The *Fortean Times'* own imprint Fortean Tomes represents some of the most solid research into the fields of lake monsters and sunken cities, whilst conspiracy theories from the Bavarian Illuminati to The Gemstone File and JFK are covered by such as Feral House. Social revolution, subversion and absurdity are side by side in a wholly natural way. Again, if alternative publishing shows us anything it is that such aspects of literature can co-exist quite happily, just as laughter, sadness and boredom do in everyday life; they don't need the artificial compartments of fiction/non-fiction, serious/humorous, classic/modern, conservative/experimental, intellectual/populist.

Directories and yearbooks

These will come into their own as tools with which to develop stock further and to identify gaps in existing alternative provision. That is not to say that they will not be useful in some instances as starting points – Byron Anderson's directory is especially useful here, if only by virtue of its size. It is compact and manageable enough not too be daunting. The comprehensiveness aimed at by Dustbooks' titles make them ideal for in-depth collection development, as well as good tools for the reference service. The following six titles are all presently continuing series, most of them updated annually.

Alternative publishers of books in North America, American Library Association, Social Responsibilities Round Table Alternatives in Print Task Force: compiled by Byron Anderson, 2nd ed.
This concise directory concentrates on the US and Canada, listing over 100 publishers deemed 'significant' by members of the Alternatives in Print Task Force. 'Significant' here means that the presses are over five years old, therefore having substantial stocklists and the reliability and reputation that come from longevity (five years is a long time in alternative publishing).

Contact details are supplemented with thumbnail sketches of each press, subjects covered, average number of titles per year and average press runs. Importantly, distributors for each press are named where these exist. A rudimentary but useful enough subject index uses similar headings to those in *APT for libraries* and covers the range of dominant subjects in alternative publishing. A small bibliography provides historical and current contexts for the state of alternative publishing in the US.

International directory of little magazines and small presses, edited by Fulton and Ferber
The American equivalent of *Small Press Yearbook*, although it covers Canada, England (*sic*) and, to a lesser extent, other English-speaking countries and a few English presses in countries such as China, Japan and the Netherlands. A single, alphabetical list of titles and publishers, this is by far the most comprehensive single reference work of its kind. There are omissions, of course; even some of the better-known alternative news titles such as *CovertAction quarterly* and *Z magazine* don't appear. Its subject index terms are broad, but useful (ecology, gay, health, human rights, political science) and it also has a regional/geographical index. An especially useful term in the subject index is 'indexes and abstracts', making this publication unique in drawing together such resources from across the whole subject range of alternative literature.

Macrocosm USA: possibilities for a new progressive era, edited by Sandi Brockway
This covers similar ground to that of the *Millenium Whole Earth*

Catalog, focusing on environmental sustainability, local community empowerment and direct democracy. It also includes many background articles reprinted from the alternative press, along with a detailed directory of over 5 000 organizations, periodicals, publishers, catalogues and other directories. Whereas the *Millenium Whole Earth Catalog* might be considered a product guide for the socially and environmentally responsible, offering some background and information for further research, *Macrocosm USA* provides in-depth contexts, information and inspiration for all aspects of the social change movements in the US. For the librarian and researcher this is an excellent single starting point for this field, since it will aid understanding and provide tools for further research and acquisition.

Magazines for Libraries, Bill and Linda Sternberg Katz
This general guide to periodical literature can be a starting point for anyone unable to get ready or immediate access to more specialist sources. Amongst its subject headings will be found 'Alternatives' and 'Little Magazines', both providing information on what could form a core collection of alternative periodicals. A number of topics found in alternative literature will also be found amongst the more usual subjects, such as civil liberties, gay and lesbian, comic books and parapsychology. Each heading also lists abstracts and indexes for each subject.

The Small Press Yearbook
This represents the most comprehensive listing of small and independent publishers in the UK. Founded in 1989 it has grown steadily in size and influence, and is now regarded by both alternative and mainstream critics as the primary source for information in this area.[4] Dependent upon small presses submitting their own information, it still managed to locate in excess of 2 000 publishers in 1994. At the heart of the book is the alphabetical listing of small presses. This includes not only alternative publishers as defined in this book, but also small, independent publishers such as the Plastics and Rubber Institute and Agricola Press (a specialist publisher of stockbreeding titles). A subject index divides publishers who have supplied categories into 25 broad

areas; less detailed indexing than appears in *Alternatives in print* (see p. 126) but effective for an overview of publishers in a specific field.

The burgeoning interest in small presses is reflected by the detailed essays that book-end the main directory. Under headings such as 'What is a Small Press?'; 'Types of Small Press'; and 'Cultural and Historical Contexts' the book can also act as a useful introduction to the philosophy and practice of independent publishing. The 'Resource Directory' at the back is aimed squarely at tyro DIY publishers who want to produce their own publications. This section includes valuable advice on starting your own press; typesetting; design and format; distribution; and legal deposit libraries.

Small press record of books in print
The alternative to *Global Books in Print*, this lists some 33 000 'books, pamphlets, broadsides, posters and poem-cards' worldwide (although a bias to the US is predictable). Over 3 000 publishers are listed. A brief (single sentence) description of each title is provided and access is by author, title, publisher and subject (the latter are of dubious value when dealing with a prolific publisher or a broad subject heading such as 'arts' or 'fiction'. Here subdivisions by medium, genre and subject matter would be helpful). There are some odd omissions: the well-known anarchist publishers AK and Black and Red do not appear, nor does the social change publisher Common Courage.

Older directories and yearbooks

The same caveat applies to the following as it does to the preceding titles: their comprehensiveness may well reserve them for the more in-depth collection development. There is much useful information on topics, titles and publishers found in these that are not to be found in any of the continuing series, but their age (or unknown status) will make this information increasingly unreliable. Many titles will be found in the *Radical Bookseller Directory* and in *From radical left to extreme right* that are not to be found in the previous titles, but which are still current. (Unfortunately to enumerate all such current listings is outwith the scope of the present work.)

Alternative publications: a guide to directories, indexes, bibliographies and other sources, edited by Cathy Seitz Whitaker
As its own introduction confirms, this small directory might be considered an updated edition of *Field guide to alternative media* (see below). It divides its sources into similar categories: indexes and abstracts, review journals, subject and trade bibliographies and alternative mail order outlets. Its coverage is mostly of the US, but it includes some Canadian sources and a few British titles. Each entry identifies the source's subject coverage, describes its layout and offers a brief critical examination of its value for the librarian. A selective bibliography of writings about alternative literature and a full index add to the worth of this title.

Alternatives in print: an international catalog of books, pamphlets, periodicals and audiovisual materials, 2nd ed.
Now sadly out of date, this final edition lists over 2500 alternative publishers worldwide. The alphabetical catalogue of publishers is supplemented by excellent indexes, which take up half of the book. These include six title indexes for each format of material (books and pamphlets, periodicals, audio recordings, films, slideshows, videotapes); an author index, a subject index to the publishers and a geographic index. Each publisher's entry contains its address and a list of its publications.

Many of the entries are still good, however (though the reader might well receive many 'return to sender' letters for every success) and its excellent subject index, using the language of the readers and writers of the publications themselves – rather than an imposed vocabulary such as LCSH – remains valuable, providing a model for appropriate subject indexing of alternative literature (this is further examined in Chapter 7).

Field guide to alternative media: a directory to reference and selection tools useful in accessing small and alternative press publications and independently produced media, edited and compiled by Patricia J. Case

This is now out of print, with no sign of a second edition (though see *Alternative publications* above). It is the only attempt – and a remarkable feat it is indeed – 'to list and describe all available [US] tools that list, index or review primarily small and alternative press publications and independently-produced media'. It comprises extensive listings of subject and trade directories, alternative review and trade journals, and bookshops and distributors' catalogues. A shorter section covers indexes and subject bibliographies. Its own bibliography is still useful, though much of the recommended reading is now of historical value only.

From radical left to extreme right: a bibliography of current periodicals of protest, controversy, advocacy, or dissent, with dispassionate content-summaries to guide librarians and other educators, 3rd ed., by Gail Skidmore and Theodore Jurgen Spahn

As its exhaustive subtitle indicates, this bibliography is aimed firmly at librarians. Despite its age it is still of value, particularly for the detailed summaries under each title. The book is arranged by general areas of interest and ideology: Marxist-socialist, liberal, conservative, peace, conservation and ecology. It is especially informative on the publications of the right, including the race supremacists, whereas most directories stay firmly on the left for their resources. Coverage of anarchist periodicals has been dropped since the previous edition (for reasons not stated).

Progressive Periodicals Directory, 2nd ed., by Craig T. Canan

This covers some 600 national US magazines, newspapers and newsletters dealing with social concerns. Each title is briefly described and entered under one of 15 headings. Most of these are similar to those used in *APT for Libraries* and include civil rights, environment, human rights and media. Although a new edition is overdue (the second edition is dated 1989), there is much here that is not covered in other directories, particularly titles in the fields of health, religion and the professions.

The Radical Bookseller Directory 1992, compiled by Einde O'Callaghan
This was the last edition produced before the demise of its founding organization, a country-wide network of radical and progressive bookshops throughout the UK and Ireland. More than a simple listing of bookshops, it also contains the only extensive listings for these islands of alternative publishers, distributors and magazines, concentrating on radical political issues, including gay and lesbian, and environmental publishing. Most of the information is still current (although there would be much to add in a new edition) and secondhand or remainder copies are worth looking out for.

Indexes

Most mainstream periodical indexes ignore the alternative press. In the UK, *British Humanities Index* indexes only the mainstream end of radical journalism, namely *New Statesman and Society*, whilst it ignores *Private Eye*. In the US the situation is slightly better. Of the mainstream indexes, *Access: the supplementary index to periodicals* indexes *Alternative Press Review, Whole Earth Review* and *Wired* amongst a majority of special interest titles. There are however two indexes that examine alternative and radical periodicals exclusively.

Alternative Press Index
This quarterly index (begun in 1969) currently indexes over 200 alternative and radical journals, magazines and newspapers, and is the prime indexing service for the alternative press, providing the only alternative to such library stalwarts as *British Humanities Index, Clover Index* and *Readers' guide to periodical literature*. There are on average 10 000 citations per issue and these include book and film reviews. Its claim to be 'the most complete index in the US to periodicals that chronicle social change' is indisputable, indeed it is the only source of its kind in the world. It covers periodicals from the US, Canada and the UK. The subject headings it uses are based on those developed by the

American Library Association's Social Responsibilities Round Table and may be considered useful for transferring to library catalogues. Any library that seriously intends to reflect social ideas at all accurately cannot afford to do without the *Alternative Press Index*.

The Left Index

'Journals selected for inclusion have a Marxist, radical or left perspective and contain lengthy, critical, analytical material' (this is crucial, since it emphasizes academic and scholarly journals). Excludes newspapers and newsletters. Includes *Dissent* but not *The Progressive*; *Mother Jones* but not *Z Magazine*, and one anarchist publication. Subjects include: economics, sociology, political science, black studies and women's studies. Main listing is by author, with indexes by subject, journal and book review.

Reference & Research Services also publish two bibliographic series, *Contemporary Social Issues* and *Social Theory*. These draw on mainstream and alternative indexes and abstracts in their compilation (including *Alternative Press Index*, *Small Press Record of Books in Print*, *Women's Studies Abstracts* and *The Left Index* itself). Each contains approximately 600 entries, including books, journal articles (academic and scholarly and general readership), government publications and pamphlets. These bibliographies are not simply subsets of *The Left Index*, since the range of titles examined for their production is wider than those for *The Left Index* itself.

Purchasing alternative publications

The larger alternative publishers such as Verso, South End Press and Black Rose Books are quite able to deal with library orders in a similar fashion to mainstream publishers. The same is true of the larger distributors: AK, Counter Productions, Fine Print, Left Bank. But since alternative publishing is a not-for-profit operation, a lack of cash flow may well require smaller publishers to ask for payment in advance of delivery. Some publishers insist on this with overseas orders, where postage cost can be punitive.

There are even a few publishers (mercifully few) that will not deal with overseas orders.

We need to remember that there are relatively few large publishers and distributors. We may well find that the items we want are only available from the author or editor themselves, who are publisher and distributor combined. Such people will not have invoicing systems and will certainly not give credit. Neither will many of them have a bank account under their press's name. Ordering details normally include a payee's name but this is not always the case. We might find ourselves faced with the prospect of writing a letter simply to ascertain a name, perhaps for an item that is hardly more than the price of postage (it does happen).

Furthermore, an individual acting as their own publisher may well have only one or two items you want, usually at low cost. Is it worth raising such an order through the finance department, when that procedure itself may well cost more than the items themselves? We need to consider alternative methods of payment, methods that are closer to personal ordering, as befits what is closer to a personal transaction. Using a cheque book (with the payee left blank, if necessary), postal orders, even cash (well-concealed) might prove to be more effective methods of paying. They will be cheaper for us, and more useful to the publisher than a cheque made to a publishing company that does not have any corporate existence; more valuable than a promise to pay within three months (your order may be enough to keep this publisher 'in business' if you pay up front). Zine publishers will often accept stamps or International Reply Coupons as payment.

Such methods of payment will also ensure that we can get hold of titles quickly. No area of alternative publishing is so changeable as the personal publisher (effectively zines), where short print runs (with no chance of reprints) are truly short; where publishers might have no intention of producing more than one title; where post office box numbers might well not be maintained beyond the life of that publication; where publishers move house. Although hardly standard purchasing tools, ready access to a cheque book and petty cash might well become indispensable to the ordering process. If your library's finance department cannot cope with this, you will need to fall back on the larger distributors and risk missing out on a vast number of titles from single-person publishers. The day when every librarian is given a personal cheque book or credit card for acquisitions purchasing is still a long way off, but when purchasing alternative literature such flexibility would be very welcome.

Acquiring alternative periodicals

For the serials librarian, the problems of periodicals are well known: changes of title and frequency; the appearance of supplementary volumes and parallel series; non-standard formats, with wildly differing standards of production. Many are not consistently indexed, storage is problematic. When we apply such criticisms to alternative periodicals we find them doubled. Frequency of publication becomes randomness or one-off. Titles might change their format, frequency and price every issue. (This not true of all: some are models of (mainstream) constancy.) There are few indexes to alternative periodicals. The very democracy of alternative literature means that the opportunities for starting your own periodical are limited only by time, imagination and budget. A new publisher or editor might use the first few issues of a periodical to learn the trade, experimenting with format, size and coverage as they proceed. *Lobster* began life as a manually typewritten photocopy: now it's professionally DTPed and printed. Some remain simple – *Zum!* is still largely handwritten and illustrated, as befits a review magazine for comics. Here this a strength of its design, being far from illegible. Some titles sport hand-coloured covers, even though their contents have left the primary school far behind. *Open Eye* sets out to be a quarterly, yet the part-time nature of the endeavour and its funding (from personal not corporate sources) has seen it publish only three issues in as many years. A year's subscription taken out in 1992 (the year of its founding) remains unexhausted at the time of writing. Claiming for unsent copies would be futile, since there aren't any. After an initial enquiry the serials librarian could only sit back and trust that future issues will arrive, eventually. But users need to know that a title as irregular as this has not ceased publication; that the issue on the shelf, ageing though it may be, is still current. Notes in the catalogue and at the shelf to this effect are essential.

It is perhaps easier to consider not stocking such a title at all, or to cancel a subscription when such irregularity becomes known. But is this a proper reason for withdrawal from stock? The absence of *Open Eye* from the newsagents' shelves is the direct result of its irregularity, where the life of an issue of any periodical will be arbitrarily cut short for commercial reasons (*Private Eye*'s 1994 supplement, *Not the Scott Report*, was only distributed and displayed by newsagents in Britain for one month, despite it continuing to remain current as the only source of much of the research in it, and certainly the only single source on the Scott Inquiry). Freed from commercial constraints, should the librarian allow such a reason to dictate their practice? A periodical issue almost two years old (as is the current issue of *Open Eye*) will hardly garner sales; even in the alternative bookshop its tattered cover bespeaks an overlooked remainder. Yet the library may safely store it and advertise its availability through the catalogue or at the shelf.

Some believe that, short of ignoring alternative periodicals and refusing to stock them because of the occasional irregular, they should be persuaded to adopt an 'industry' standard. This has been recently promoted as a serious answer to what is regarded by the UK Serials Group as profligate and irresponsible periodicals production. In its *Serial publications: guidelines for good practice in publishing printed journals and other serial publications*,[5] a joint working group attempts to dictate to journal publishers how their publications should be laid out and numbered. It even includes recommendations for choosing a title (!). But those involved in alternative publishing are no less aware of these problems, as well as the advantages, that such diverse and democratic forms can bring. The rationale behind this book has had to take these problems into account, for which it has been necessary to be highly selective yet still representative of the immense range of alternative publications. Some see that diversity as, if not a weakness, then as an opportunity for consolidation. Michael Albert of *Z Magazine* has recommended the launching of a national alternative weekly newspaper for the US which would integrate the existing expertise and resources of many already involved in the production of their own (less frequent) newspapers and magazines. This has been supported by Noam Chomsky, although it has caused concern in some quarters. Freedom Press noted in 1990 that the Centre International de Recherches sur L'Anarchisme at Lausanne had in a few months received 40 anarchist periodicals in English. It too calls for consolidation: 'how easy it would be if all the effort and money put into producing these 40 journals was used to produce an International (*sic*) anarchist weekly.'[6] At the heart of both these calls is not monopoly and control, but the most effective use of people and resources in areas of endeavour that have always relied on voluntary labour and limited funds. Pooling such resources, it is argued, would not only improve research and news gathering activities, it would also give a higher profile to the single alternative journal and the promotion of alternative ideas to the public. This is unlikely to happen – the fierce independence of many in alternative publishing is too much for that. Networking and cooperation may well be common amongst participants, but relinquishing one's own titles is not a popular option. If we are to rely on anything it is an increase, not a decline, in the number of alternative periodical titles. But an opposite view is equally strong amongst the alternative media, one that considers the proliferation of titles as a democratic strength: 'One hundred publications with a circulation of one thousand are one hundred times better than one publication with a circulation of one hundred thousand'.[7]

References

1. *Magazines for Libraries*, New Providence, NJ: R.R. Bowker, 1992, p. 93.
2. 'Reference Review', *Librarians at Liberty*, **2**(1), 16.
3. *Politically controversial monographs: roles of publishers, distributors, booksellers, Choice magazine, and librarians in acquiring*

them for academic libraries, Building on the first century: proceedings of the Fifth National Conference of the Association of College and Research Libraries, Cincinnati, Ohio, April 5–8, 1989, Association of College and Research Libraries, 1989, 238–41.

4. At the time of writing the uncertain future of the Yearbook's parent body, the Small Press Group of Britain and its National Small Press Centre at Middlesex University leaves future editions in doubt.

5. Witney: UK Serials Group, 1994.

6. Freedom Press, 'Discussion notes on communicating', *The Raven* 3(4), October-December 1990, pp. 377–83.

7. November's 'thought' from 'Another year of the same old shit: calendar 1995', Oxford: Institute of Social Disengineering, 1994.

6 Strategies for Current Awareness

The fluid and transient nature of much alternative publishing is such that many enterprises are often short-lived, and many may take years to fulfil their promise. Furthermore, there is no guarantee that today's best source for alternative information will not disappear. In addition, many of the most incisive and rewarding alternative publications are one-offs: the result of a single author-publisher's obsession with a subject, that might need no further publications to make its point. Here the venture into publishing was in order to circulate an author's ideas rather than to establish a publishing company to compete with commercial interests. On the other hand, many long-lived publications have declined in interest and quality as they have put increasingly unbearable pressures on their editors and publishers, who strive to continue with them in the face of financial crisis and pressures of personal life and full-time work. Remember that most people working in alternative publishing are there out of love or commitment: as a rule they earn a living elsewhere.

The short-lived nature of many alternative publishing ventures makes the need for current awareness crucial. But not only must we keep abreast of the publications that appear, we also need to be able to act upon the information we receive. Short print runs and narrow channels of distribution mean that a title may well go out of print quickly, often with little chance of reprinting. Fast and efficient ordering is essential, but this will entail different strategies from those that most librarians employ.

The importance of networking

Networking as practised within the alternative milieu might be thought of as practical anarchy: leaderless, decentralized. Instead of information being passed to a central point from where it is distributed (and consequently filtered or repackaged) it passes straight to the people who want it. They then pass it on through further networks, returning their own information back along the same channels. Central points do at times arise at nodes where a number of channels intersect. It is at these that distributors operate, and where bibliographies and review journals appear. These do not attempt to impede the flow nor do they seek to impose a structure on it, rather they simply log its existence and send bulletins throughout the networks to increase people's knowledge of the already existing information.

This is what has been called 'many-to-many' communication, superseding the previously dominant modes of one-to-many (mass media) and one-to-one (face-to-face and written personal communication). The concept of many-to-many communication has been most enthusiastically propounded by the gurus of the Internet, yet it is hardly a new thing, as the networks of the alternative printed media attest.

Networking is central in alternative publishing. It comprises all manner of interpenetrating networks, where everyone involved becomes informed by one another, whether they are in agreement or not: 'vibrant networks working out new cultural fronts in co-operation and opposition', as Luke McGuff has it. He goes on to make a point that is obvious to all involved in alternative publishing: 'It's a culture of participation [and] cultures of participation are inherently invisible to non-participants.'[1] This provides another reason why so much alternative literature goes unregarded by libraries and the mainstream media.

Librarians who want to become more than merely acquainted with alternative literature need some way of participating in these networks, for it is only through such involvement that we can truly come to understand the workings of alternative publishing. Equally importantly, such involvement will enable us to keep our knowledge up to date in a field where there are few updating and current awareness tools (as we have seen). Information about new titles and publishers, the disappearance of some and the change of titles and addresses of others: much of this information will come through such networks. By getting on the inside of the networks, we will also be present as new topics and new views arise. Consequently we will be able to develop our collections and our information sources timeously.

Given the diversity of alternative publishing and its continually shifting nature, such a project is essential. But such a project might also seem doomed to failure, or to rejection. For who, after all, can afford the time to apparently immerse themselves in such work, when so many other tasks are also crying out for our attention? In an age where cost-effectiveness appears to have replaced the imperative of finding and disseminating the widest possible sources of information and knowledge – to say nothing of the marginalization of our social responsibilities – how can we justify such an extravagance? Of course it is not an extravagance at all – no more extravagant than entertaining commercial representatives or visiting high street bookshops or suppliers' showrooms – yet for pragmatic reasons we should perhaps venture into such a project gradually. Once the benefits become clear to us and our users we can then embark on more thoroughgoing assays into the world of networking. There is no doubt that benefits will accrue. The present book has been entirely sourced by networking through the alternative press and by working with people involved in it.

What follows is therefore preparatory in nature, but contains within it the seeds for much more rigorous explorations. Let us begin by identifying two basic methods: networking by way of the literature itself and networking with the people involved in alternative publishing.

Networking through the literature

At its most basic level this need entail no more than close reading of information sources such as those discussed in the previous chapter. Yet becoming assiduous readers of titles like *Factsheet 5* and *Alternative Press Review* is only the beginning. Since it is largely untrammelled by commercial and competitive forces, and is less concerned about providing free publicity to what in the mainstream would be called 'rival interests', the periodical literature of the alternative press is far more committed to the dissemination of information and ideas than that of the mainstream. Not only is such publicity offered, much more of a periodical's pages will be taken up by such publicity. Many alternative periodicals will typically devote far many more pages to reviews than their mainstream counterparts, just as they will include extensive lists of organizations, publishers, other periodicals and other sources of information. All this is essential material for networking.

Sometimes the impact of this type of close reading can produce unexpected effects. It was a reference at the end of an article in an issue of *Lobster* that led to the founding of the activist librarians' group Information for Social Change, through byways too tortuous to map here. Suffice to say, were it not for *Lobster* then *Information for Social Change* would not exist. *Lobster* is a model for the potential to be found in this kind of networking. To begin with, the research it presents is nothing if not rigorous. In the field of parapolitics, where so much writing can easily drift into unfounded speculation, annotated articles are crucial. Most are accompanied by dozens of closely-typed footnotes, bibliographies and suggestions for further reading. An issue of *Lobster* is more than a record of current research. It can be used as a reference source, a review journal and a significant networking tool to access a whole other world of ideas, publications and people. Consider the contents of issue 26 of Robin Ramsay's *Lobster*.

The opening article by Daniel Brandt, 'Cyberspace wars', in addition to its value as a counter to the prevailing media representations of the Internet, also examines the activities of right-wing pressure groups such as Western Goals and the Anti-Defamation League (B'nai Brith). It reports on the work of the groups Computer Professionals for Social Responsibility and the Electronic Frontier Foundation. He tells us about NameBase, a tool that he recommends for both investigative journalists and reference libraries. For many readers this will be the first time they have encountered such names. Elsewhere in the same issue we find reviews of almost 50 recent books dealing with the assassination of President Kennedy along with eight pages of book reviews on other topics. Scattered throughout the rest of the issue, often in footnotes, we find the names and addresses of organizations, publications and individuals, all involved in parapolitical research. But *Lobster* is not unique: *Anarchy* regularly reviews in excess of 100 publications in each issue; the first issue of *Promises and Disappointments* reviewed an equivalent number across the spectrum of paranormal, Fortean and UFO research publications. The practice of mailing out fliers, broadsheets, even others publishers' free zines with one's own work is commonplace. The current favourite for this practice, which seems to appear in every mailing received by the author during the writing of this book, is a reprint of Ivan Schcheglov's Situationist tract *Formulary for a new urbanism*, circulated by the London Psychogeographical Association/Unpopular Books. The author's copy of the latest edition of *Light's List* came in an envelope stuffed with fliers and mini-catalogues for chapbooks, poetry and short story magazines and zines. Alternative publishers cooperate endlessly in their networking, which is all to the benefit of anyone researching or acquiring. You will very soon find yourself part of a network, receiving unexpected, unsolicited mail from publishers you never knew existed, publishing titles on topics you never dreamed of.

You can either throw your hands up in despair at the perverse diversity of it all or you can dive in, safe in knowing that even if you never plumb its depths, you will always return with something – maybe even the odd pearl. You will never find all there is to be found, you cannot even chart it all. But a brief dip will retrieve something and might leave you wanting to dive deeper next time.

Electronic networking

We have already looked at the potential of the Internet as an information source and a supplier of alternative publications. The potential of a tool like the World Wide Web goes further than simple identification and retrieval. If alternative publishing may be thought of as (in Bob Black's words) 'a web of relationships' that flourishes through 'cross-pollination', then the World Wide Web surely emulates this dynamic through its hyperlinks. Locating a single WWW home page will inevitably point you to other home pages, other sources of information. Some will be of direct relevance to the object of your initial search, others will take you serendipitously to topics and places unintended and unexpected.

Chuck Munson is the editor of *Practical Anarchy* and the owner of the Mid-Atlantic Infoshop Home Page. In addition to providing access to *Practical Anarchy Online* and a directory of info-shops and bookshops (mostly US at present, but European locations are being added), it gives access to *MSRRT Newsletter* and provides links to NativeNet, Spunk Press, *Factsheet 5 Electric* and *Whole Earth Review*. There is a link to an ongoing index to electronic journals and zines and to The Seed, an embryonic gateway to information on alternative publishing in the UK, providing links to Freedom Press, the European Counter Network (including articles from *Contraflow*) and the full text of the *Anarchist Yearbook*. Still on the Mid-Atlantic Infoshop Home Page a section headed 'Resources of Interest to Activists' will link you to, amongst others, a 'critical mass' page giving details of cycle campaigns in Europe and North America (this page will take you to Velonet, the Global Cycling Network). One of the providers of this information is Nick Fiddes, a social anthropologist at the University of Edinburgh, whose own page is accessible here. He provides the products of his research into environmental and animal rights activism here, including an encyclopaedia of direct action and updates about protests against the Criminal Justice Act, the UK's road-building programme and the latest news on the 'McLibel' trial. Articles from *Earth First! Journal* are also available. His 'Reference Desk' includes searchable copies of *Webster's Dictionary*, a dictionary of acronyms, a currency converter and direct links to Scottish library OPACs and the Scottish Academic Libraries Serials database. He also provides direct links to the newsgroups misc.activism.progressive and alt.activism. Finally he offers a link to Eric Lease Morgan's reference desk and the *Virtual Reference Desk* gopher, which together contain hundreds of links to library catalogues, electronic journals, dictionaries and encyclopaedias. All from Chuck Munson's simple, single home page.

Networking with publishers

Many alternative publishers and distributors are eager to establish a relationship with other people in the information world, especially when it comes to getting their titles into libraries. In the author's experience requests for information are considered with an enthusiasm often understandably absent from the larger, conglomerate publishers, due to pressures of time. No doubt as small publishers grow they too will find themselves being able to devote less time to personal contacts, but for now many will be happy to engage in correspondence beyond the mere mailing of a catalogue. Personal contact is often at a premium in our encounters with publishers and distributors and especially useful in an area where we might still be finding our way. It is worth bearing in mind that the person representing the alternative publisher may also well be one of its main authors, editors or layout artists. They may well be able to tell you as much about the ethos and processes of alternative publishing as they can about their stocklist. They will also be able to act as a guide to other areas of alternative publishers: most of these people are dedicated networkers, indeed, it is by developing such networks that they might well have decided to enter publishing themselves. Since these people are all in the same, low profit, low kudos business, working out of love, out of commitment to a cause or towards a desideratum beyond the merely economic, they will show little rivalry. It is in their interests to promote alternative publishing as a whole. Anything they can do to increase its profile will benefit their own work, even if that means recommending other publishers and distributors to their customers.

In return librarians can offer useful information about how to do business with their libraries. On more than one occasion librarians have been accused of being secretive and obstructive about their selection (and deselection) policies.[2] Those publishers who are not geared up for library supply would find a chat or even an information sheet about the library's policies very beneficial. If we are serious about incorporating this literature into our collections we must also be serious about accepting it on its own terms. However desirous inspection copies and credit terms might be to librarians and their finance departments, if we insist on these requirements and procedures from publishers not set up to offer them, then we will do nothing but drive them away. Flexibility is the key. Many small publishers have little understanding of how to approach libraries with their stock; many assume that their material would not be suitable in some way. Librarians should do all they can to disabuse publishers of such notions. If they are unable to stock it, then their reasons should be clear, honest and justifiable, and not a simple reiteration of the standard 'there's no demand for it'.

Networking with local groups

Networking has a further value at a local level. Local interest groups and local groups representing regional, national or international interests can often prove to be valuable sources of information for publications, both those produced by their own groups and by others with similar interests. Many of these groups will have their own regular newsletter or journal, which can certainly be considered for stock; a group may well offer you a free subscription to such an item. In many groups, particularly campaigning groups such as World Development Movement and Campaign Against Arms Trade, there is an emphasis on self-education: members often research aspects of their interest to present to the rest of the group, take part in public meetings and produce handouts and leaflets. Groups often establish their own small 'libraries' of relevant books, periodicals and papers, sometimes in collaboration with a local alternative bookshop or information centre.

The rise of the 'infoshop' in recent years throughout Europe and the US is one manifestation of such local activity. Usually based around a local anarchist group, although it is of benefit to more than anarchists, it acts as a communication and distribution point for any number of local, national and international groups, movements and projects. It can function as an archive of community information for local activists, as a meeting place and a resource centre. Some infoshops provide the only public access service to the Internet, along with cheap computing, layout and copying facilities. Many newspapers, pamphlets and zines are produced using the resources of an infoshop, some even use it as a mailing address. It is often the only place in a town that can always supply the latest information on environmental, peace and human rights campaigns, and acts as the focus of an alert network for local activists in these areas. The infoshop emphasizes empowerment, providing information freely (or very cheaply) to enable people to work together, directly, on issues that affect their lives. Since the infoshop can be so central to so many people, its existence will be well-publicized, both through the literature it promotes and through local notice-boards in radical bookshops, cafés and other alternative meeting places. Infoshops are often found in the same premises as food cooperatives and cafés. Infoshops are regularly listed in the anarchist press and in *Bypass*. Chuck Munson's Mid-Atlantic Infoshop Home Page will eventually provide information on (and even some links to) infoshops throughout North America and Europe.

The Free Information Network (FIN) in the UK is a corollary to the infoshop. It grew out of the free festival movement in the UK,

in order to publicize such events, along with news of demonstrations and actions that tended to be ignored by the mass media.
There are now many FINs throughout the UK, each usually producing its own 'FIN-news', a newssheet of local events of these
types. New FINs are continually appearing, but the most recent
list of them appears in *Bypass* 4.

Alternative libraries and archives

Finding that so few mainstream libraries stock alternative publications, there a few individuals and groups who have set up
their own archives and libraries to ensure that these publications
are collected and made available to the public.

In the US there have opened recently a number of alternative
libraries, providing reading room space along with a basic reference enquiry service. The Alternative Reading Room in Ashville,
North Carolina, describes itself as 'an activist library of materials
on the environment, social and political issues, peace, religion
and atheism, news and culture'. It aims to complement local
libraries by acquiring material they do not stock, either because
they cannot identify it, find it or afford it, or because it is considered 'controversial'. Its 250 magazine subscriptions are the centrepiece of the collection.[3]

The Civic Media Center and Library was set up in Gainesville,
Florida to 'provide access to information and points of view not
carried or incompletely carried by the for-profit, corporate
media'. It focuses on social and environmental issues and
actively seeks to stock titles which are not available in other local
libraries.[4] Silid Aklatan (Philippine dialect meaning 'room of
books') is a mail-order library of anarchist books and pamphlets.
It operates on trust and cooperation, loaning items for open peri-
ods, for the price of postage only.

In the UK we will find The Commonweal Collection, dedicated to the acquisition of materials related to the peace movement. It was established in 1958 and is housed in the J.B.
Priestley Library at the University of Bradford, comprising some
10000 books and periodicals focusing on pacifism, peace educa-

tion and the promotion of non-violent social change. It also 'probably contains the most comprehensive collection of works on Gandhi in the UK' (according to its promotional leaflet). True to the spirit of many alternative libraries, it is entirely open to the public and offers free borrowing facilities to all.

The aim of the Kate Sharpley Library and Documentation Centre is to function as the primary archive and library for anarchism, focusing on the UK but including materials from abroad where they have had an impact on the development of anarchism in the UK. It is made up of private donations and comprises several thousand books, newspapers, journals and pamphlets, in addition to posters, flyers, videos and unpublished manuscripts. Due to storage problems – coupled with the subversive and confidential nature of much of the material – the library does not have public access, save by appointment. Even its location is kept secret, and applicants must write c/o the BM number to arrange a visit. It is run solely by volunteers, which explains why its massive retrospective cataloguing project is extremely behind schedule. It does, however, provide a rudimentary reference service and will supply, for instance, photocopies of known items from the prominent anarchist journal *Black Flag* where available (and on payment). The library has perhaps taken on more than it can hope to achieve: it also runs a publishing programme, currently comprising 13 titles. Its bulletin *KSL* is available on subscription and provides updates of the cataloguing project, along with extracts from its extensive archives. The bulletin will also publish its catalogue listings as they become available (the first of these will be its English book list). The Anarchist Archives Project works in a similar way, relying on donations of material which it collects and catalogues, making its collection of around 10 000 periodicals, books, pamphlets and newspaper clippings available to researchers, and offering photocopy facilities, the compilation of bibliographies and (limited) personal access.

Centres such as infoshops and alternative libraries offer plenty of scope for collaborative projects between local libraries and infoshops. If we are looking for expertise and knowledge in tracing and acquiring alternative publications, the volunteers who run such centres are worth talking to. Such are the quantities of material they have acquired, in fact, that they might well be glad of our expertise to organize it.

But do we need to duplicate their efforts in the library? If an infoshop or an alternative library exists, why bother stocking alternative literature at all? We should bear in mind that alternative libraries are rare (rarer than infoshops, which seem to be on the increase across Europe and North America). They tend to exist on donations alone (both stock and money), but since their users and supporters tend to come from low incomes they do not enjoy anything like the funding that even the cash-straitened local public library does. Why not consolidate around co-promotion and mutual support? The library might decide to buy the stock the other cannot afford, supplemented by a core collection based on the infoshop's wider collection. Remember that opening hours might well vary. The infoshop and alternative library will operate only with volunteer staff; evening and weekend opening are rare. But we should not ignore alternative literature simply because there is an infoshop in town. Bear in mind that the infoshop, just like the tourist office and the business information centre, is catering to a specific community – there will be areas of alternative provision that even it cannot be expected to cover. Collaboration and networking are crucial to exploit existing resources and to identify their shortfalls.

The alternative library has surely reached its apogee at the Brautigan Library in Burlington, Vermont, which exists solely to house unpublished books. Authors of all ages and from all walks of life are encouraged to donate their home-made books and manuscripts, which are then catalogued and shelved. People visit the library simply for the pleasure of seeing their own work on its shelves; there are no selection criteria, save that every work must be unpublished. The library draws its inspiration from Richard Brautigan's novel *The abortion: an historical romance 1966*, the protagonist of which is the librarian of a unique collection of unpublished works in San Francisco: 'This library came into being because of an overwhelming need and desire for such a place. There just simply had to be a library like this.'[5] Brautigan's humanist, egalitarian conceit has been made flesh in what some might term a 'vanity' library. But giving unpublished authors a voice goes well beyond vanity. It aims to provide an outlet for the unpublished and the unpublishable, a conduit for the creative energy so often bottled up in a world where only a few (relatively speaking) are accorded the privilege of becoming published authors.

Alternative bookshops

The mushrooming of alternative bookshops in the US and Britain of the 1970s grew out of the political activism of the 1960s and reached its peak in the following decade. For most of that period they were havens for the numberless varieties of communist thought. Never sound commercial propositions at the best of times, they became increasingly difficult to run as the economic climate turned against small, independent businesses and national and international companies began assimilating the more popular titles into their own stock. As rents rose, more shops were forced out of the town centres and into back alleys. The number of such bookshops has decreased alarmingly in Britain – there are hardly more than a dozen outside London. Those remaining hang on by virtue of their wider radical interests, reflecting social concerns such as environmental responsibility, Third World issues, sexual politics and alternative ways of living. These have been their lifeblood, as communities of interest find themselves not so much through minority political movements but through wider social movements. In the UK these shops have been attempting to interest libraries in their stock, with varying degrees of success. Whilst Edinburgh's gay bookshop West and Wilde and Manchester's Frontline do enjoy a few orders from local libraries, Nottingham's Mushroom declares that it has been trying for 20 years to get its books into libraries with no success. Such failure is odd, since the alternative bookshop is often the only showcase for many alternative titles. If we are unlikely to see such titles in other bookshops and in the showrooms of library suppliers, the alternative bookshop can provide us with a unique opportunity to assess titles and topics unknown to us. It strength here is twofold. It will stock a range of specialist titles (politics, poetry, diverse journals) as well as being of value for supplementing general library collections (fiction, children's books, green, women's issues). In common with the infoshop and the alternative library, the alternative bookshop can provide specialist knowledge and access to the world of alternative publishing. It can not only provide a quick and efficient service for titles not in stock, but also advise librarians on identifying and selecting stock from a range of unfamiliar publishers and distributors.

Alternative librarians

So far we have only looked at libraries, information sources, groups and individuals that are outwith the mainstream, that do not form part of the librarian's usual milieu. Yet as we noted in the previous chapter a number of librarians have been and continue to be the prime movers in publicizing and disseminating alternative literature by publishing their own, independent bibliographies and review journals. As librarians they will have experience of the peculiar challenges that identifying, acquiring and managing alternative literature will bring. Making contact with such people may provide fruitful cooperation and mutual support in what otherwise might be a lonely occupation. There are a number of publications and organizations run by such 'activist librarians'. Whether you think of yourself as an activist or not, the decision to acquire alternative literature is very much a demonstrative move, a significant act that has led to the politicization of at least one librarian.

In addition to publishing *APT for Libraries* under his CRISES Press imprint, Charles Willett publishes a twice-yearly 'interactive newsletter', *Librarians at Liberty*, that provides a forum for librarians working with alternative literature and issues of social justice, censorship and freedom of information to share views, ideas and problems. Presented in approachable, non-specialist language, it is very amenable to new readers and an invaluable networking tool. The Progressive Librarians' Guild publishes its own quarterly journal *Progressive Librarian*, examining issues of censorship and freedom through longer, more detailed articles. The American Library Association's Social Responsibilities Round Table (and its regional offshoots such as the Minnesota Social Responsibilities Round Table, the publisher of *MSRRT Newsletter*) aims to heighten awareness about many of the issues surrounding library provision that are discussed in this book through meetings and publications. The UK's Library Association unfortunately has no such forum and there is only one independent group that is trying to cover all aspects of such issues that a range of US groups and journals spread amongst themselves. Through its twice-yearly journal of the same name, Information for Social Change promotes alternatives to mainstream library provision, debates issues of ethics, freedom of information and censorship, and examines the roles of the librarian within society. Such groups are in turn part of the international network including the Library and Information Workers' Organisation of South Africa and the Arbeitskreis Critische Bibliothekarinnen of Germany.

References

1. In a review of 'Covert Culture Sourcebook', *Alternative Press Review* **2**, Winter 1994, p. 81.
2. Fred Whitehead's 'What ever happened to the rare books?' (*Journal of Information Ethics* 2(2), Fall 1993, pp. 11–14, reprinted in *Information for Social Change* (1), Winter 1994, pp. 10–13) and the *Report of the PEN Committee on Censorship* (London: English Centre of International PEN, 1993) are but two.
3. Paula E. Davidson, 'Activist library celebrates third year', *Librarians at Liberty*, **1**(2), January 1994, pp. 4–5 and Liz Enochs, 'Selections from the edge: the Alternative Reading Room leans both ways', *Alternative Press Review* **2**, Winter 1994, pp. 8–9.
4. Charles Willett, 'Starting an alternative library', *Librarians at Liberty* **1**(2), January 1994, pp. 6–7.

5. Richard Brautigan, *The abortion: an historical romance 1966* (New York, NY: Simon and Schuster Pocket Books, 1972), p. 21.

7 Aspects of Collection Management

Storage: scatter *versus* concentration

It is possible to treat alternative literature as a special collection, much as libraries treat community information or local history collections. The organization and storage of alternative literature separate from the main body of the library may be justified in a number of ways. Librarians expecting controversy and complaint after acquiring non-mainstream material which promotes unfamiliar ideas might prefer to secrete it safely away. Since this will reduce the number of casual browsers, it is argued, there is less likelihood of it offending people (this argument assumes that people will be offended by anything unfamiliar to them). In much the same way are 'adult' (soft porn) videos shelved separately in video shops. But to do so is to encourage a return to the bad old days of the catalogue entry marked 'Kept in Librarian's Office', formerly reserved for soft porn and sex education books. Having taken steps to acquire alternative publications, so often marginalized by the mainstream media and high street bookshops, are we then to marginalize them in our libraries by making access less than open? It may also be argued that if such material is acquired with a special group of users in mind, they may well prefer to have 'their' titles housed together. Yet, as we have seen throughout this book, alternative literature does not exist separately from that of the mainstream. It comments upon it, it supplements it. It is surely more appropriate for alternative and mainstream to co-exist, for them to be able to inform one another by being housed together as part of a larger collection, than for alternative literature to remain in a ghetto that hardly represents its true place in the world of ideas. Its function as a counter to the dominant views, opinions and 'facts' on library shelves throughout the world needs to be assessed in relation to the mainstream itself. To do this most effectively such materials should enjoy neither the special privilege of the special collection, nor the ghettoization that such a collection might equally offer. They need to exist in the same space and on equal terms with the materials they are there to counter, to criticize, to enhance. The alternative newspaper should enjoy equal visibility and equal 'respectability' to the mainstream newspaper. The book criticizing the mass media and exposing its propaganda techniques should be there on the shelf alongside the book that fêtes the freedom of the press in the West, at the same time as it ridicules the crude propaganda systems of the rest of the world's state-controlled media. By co-existing, each stands or falls on its merits; each will be seen in the light of the other; and the library user seeking information on topic x – whether from a critical viewpoint or no – will find everything on that subject at a single location.

It might be argued that alternative literature that is acquired in order to function as a kind of local alternative community information collection should be housed separately, or as part of an existing collection of community information. But when other, general alternative information is acquired the librarian is faced with another dilemma. Since it would make no sense to house it with the existing local information, should it also be given status as another special collection? The librarian runs the risk of making the library into a plethora of special collections. The virtual library predicted by some commentators is far from near; for many librarians the integrated, automated catalogue is a luxury they are only just planning for. A library founded on separate collections might well remain a library separated.

Even with an effective, integrated catalogue, much library use is still based on browsing. Having to first decide on the most appropriate section to browse in is yet another barrier to serendipity, especially if a collection is labelled with such a term as 'alternative' which, outside its use in a book such as this, can have an entirely ambiguous meaning to the library user. The special collection might also encourage different storage and retrieval practices – a particular temptation given the many idiosyncratic features of much alternative literature. In fact, given that many titles are non-standard in format, some librarians believe that alternative literature is most appropriately stored in similar fashion to much grey literature, using vertical files, pamphlet boxes and cabinets. The corollary is that such methods require their own retrieval systems or, at best, an additional step in the retrieval process from master catalogue to special collection. This ensures that they will only be used by either the most persistent user or the researcher. As soon as storage becomes an obstacle to browsing usage will decrease. In this respect such items must endure the same fate as 'grey literature', although many unspined, stapled, 'non-standard' items will often have an intellectual content and a literary value to equal that of the professionally-produced hardback or perfect-bound paperback.

Some librarians prefer not to acquire alternative titles since they believe that 'controversial' materials have a history of theft and defacement. To then withdraw the stock from public view and prevent independent, unmediated public access is hardly satisfactory. To enable these materials to flourish, to do the job for which we have acquired them, they need to be out there with the rest of the stock.

This is not to say that alternative literature should not be treated as a special area of library provision, that it should not be maintained with care. As with a special collection, alternative literature could hope to have its own specialist librarian – possibly buyer, cataloguer and reader services librarian combined. James Danky believes that a librarian, 'should choose his or her own

subject to become an expert on ... For if you know something –
and by that I mean that you are steeped in the literature ... then
you will attract the respect and admiration that all librarians
strive to attain.'[1] Establishing a collection of alternative materials
is one way of fostering the expertise that Danky sees as essential
to redress the balance between – and begin once more 'honoring'
– 'stuff over process'. There is no reason for that collection to
remain physically separate from the library's mainstream provision. As a first step, having one librarian in sole charge of acquiring the alternative literature will be an asset. That librarian will
need to work closely with other staff, since decisions about
acquisitions will be informed by the mainstream stock as much
as by other alternative stock. Similarly decisions about cataloguing and classification will also need to be made jointly. Once the
policy and practice of acquiring and managing alternative literature has become established there is no reason why the procedures cannot be incorporated into general library provision.
Having a librarian with expertise in the field will enable other
staff to be easily introduced to the literature and trained in its
methods of acquisition and management. In due course this
should lead to the acquisition of alternative literature becoming
a natural, integrated part of library provision.

Storage within a main collection: the problems of format

It is easy to over-estimate the storage problems of alternative literature and to forget that most of it is produced in formats that
should cause no serious difficulties for storage. In common with
grey literature its presentation might be basic, but that should
give no cause for its rejection from stock. Many alternative publications look no different from commercial perfect-bound paper-
backs, whilst the majority of zines and pamphlets will be A4 or
A5 staple-bound and photocopied, commonly with single-
colour card or stiff paper covers. These are hardly radical binding and design techniques, however 'unprofessional' they might
appear. Perhaps it is in the comparison with the products of com

mercial publishers that alternative publications most suffer. To the librarian and the user familiar with glossy dustjackets and high-quality paper and printing, many alternative publications will have little appeal. Yet through familiarity librarians and users will come to appreciate these differences or see beyond them to the contents within (do we need to restate the cliché about how never to judge a book?). To discriminate on the grounds of format and presentation could well mean fragment-ing the coverage of a subject purely on the grounds of format. (This is already a familiar occurrence in mixed-media collec-tions, but no less justifiable for that.) The hidden message is: if the item is up to 'standard' it will be accorded the privilege of display with its mainstream peers. But whose standard? And for whose benefit?

Consider the audiences at whom such publications are aimed. One of the aims of acquiring alternative publications is to increase the relevance of our libraries to infrequent and non-users. A further aim might be to actively encourage them to par-ticipate in developing library services to communities hitherto ignored or marginalized. To achieve such aims entails stocking titles whose content and nature might be unfamiliar to us. We should not then blanch if these same titles possess design and production values that might not concord with our own.

However, problems of storage will arise with 'non-standard' formats such as A6 and A7 booklets (a few A8 items do exist, but most appear in 'multimedia kits' containing prints, booklets, recorded music and loose-leaf pages). These will inevitably fall behind shelves, be easily damaged or simply never be seen even by the most assiduous browser. Such items can be housed in a larger document wallet or a portfolio binder. A set of titles such as Playtime For Ever Press's A6 booklets could be conveniently stored as a collection in an audio cassette shelf storage box.

Single sheet publications such as *The Bug* are less common, but both it and a publication such as the *Scum Directory*, amounting to a handful of A4 sheets stapled at one corner, are liable to befall similar fates. Such publications can easily be laminated and, if necessary, spiral bound (they will be more secure than in ring binders). This will not only preserve them but give them a stronger presence on the shelf and make them more immune to theft. Occasionally we will find publications that have decorated covers, whether collages of the types that adorn the women's zine *Heavy Flow* or the sandpaper sheets of *An endless adventure ... an endless passion ... an endless banquet: a situationist scrapbook*. The first is susceptible to damage itself, the second would cause significant damage to any items it was shelved between. The answer in both cases is straightforward: a plastic slip-on cover will protect the item and any others near it.

Improving access through cataloguing

Access hardly stops at dealing with unusual formats. The cataloguing and classification of such materials can also provide challenges, calling for imagination and insight. In the author's experience these qualities are signally lacking in the bulk of Cataloguing-in-Publication (CIP) data produced by the British Library and the Library of Congress. Alternative titles that deal with unusual or novel subject matter are often classified inadequately. The consequent assigning of appropriate and relevant subject headings to these titles will then be equally inadequate.

The bulk of alternative publications will have no CIP data at all, since they have bypassed the bibliographic systems that entail such documentation. Here the problems are doubled. However inadequate CIP data might be, it does at least provide a starting point. The traditional lack of reliable CIP data for those alternative materials that possess it means that even previously acquired items are of little use as models, unless their catalogue records have been substantially modified. To this must be added the bibliographic vagaries of much alternative publishing. Robert Lynn's pamphlet *Vote: what for?* has no place of publication, no publisher and no date. *The heretic's guide to the Bible*, published by Irate Press, has no place of publication, no date and no author. The tendency might be to catalogue such items only as far as the information allows, whereas a more analytical extensive approach would improve the meaningfulness of the catalogue record and the traceability of the item by the user.

Sanford Berman, chief cataloguer at Hennepin County Library, remains one of the prime movers to reform cataloguing practice. Although he has focused on alternative materials insofar as they provide new and unconsidered subject matter, his recommendations could be equally applied to mainstream publications. After decades of lobbying, Berman's efforts to persuade the Library of Congress to incorporate subject headings into its cataloguing records that are meaningful to users is finally proving successful. His books *Prejudices and antipathies: a tract on the LC Subject Heads concerning people* and *Worth noting: editorials, letters, essays, an interview and bibliography* document his sustained struggle. He has consistently developed headings that are based on the subject matter and language in the documents themselves, rather than on an artificially and arbitrarily adopted vocabulary. His headings reflect the language of the communities and cultures that have produced such items rather than that of a professional élite (librarians) that may well be out of touch with the people and the publications they read.

In his contribution to *Alternative materials in libraries* Berman recommends the following simple steps, the adoption of even just one of which would improve catalogue access significantly. The library that adopts them all on all available occasions would improve access immeasurably.

1. Make added entries for sponsoring, producing or otherwise closely associated presses, groups, agencies and provide 'public notes' to briefly identify these groups.
2. Make added entries for subtitles and catch-titles that users may remember and seek.
3. Impose no upper limit on subject tracings, applying as many as necessary to substantially and accurately reflect the content of a given work.
4. Assign subject tracings to fiction on the same basis as non-fiction.
5. Reform biased, imprecise, awkward or antique subject descriptors that misrepresent, defame or 'bury' the topics they ostensibly denote.
6. Establish new descriptors.

7.   Compose notes to clarify contents, indicate special features and show relationships to other works, persons or groups.[2]

Berman has devised what he calls 'Alternative Cataloguing-in-Publication Data' which accompanies Library of Congress Cataloging Data on the title page verso of any book by Berman or in which he is involved. The results of such practices are startling to anyone used to the conventional CIP data. Below are the two records as they appear in Berman and Danky's *Alternative Library Literature, 1992/1993: a biennial anthology* (Figures 7.1 and 7.2):

Alternative library literature: a biennial anthology.—1982/1983–

   v. : ill. ; 28 cm.

Biennial.
Includes index.
Edited by Sanford Berman and James P. Danky, 1982/1983–
ISSN 0749-6885 = Alternative library literature.

1. Libraries and society — Addresses, essays, lectures. 2. Underground   press — Addresses, essays, lectures. 3. Anti-nuclear movement — Addresses, essays, lectures. 4. Women in library science — Addresses, essays, lectures. 5. Library science — Addresses, essays, lectures. I. Berman, Sanford, 1933– . II. Danky, James Philip, 1947–

   Z716.4.A47   020'.5 – dc19   84–646841

                        AACR2 MARC-S

Figure 7.1   Library of Congress Cataloguing Data for Berman and Danky's *Alternative Library Literature, 1992/1993: a biennial anthology*

Alternative library literature: a biennial anthology.
   1982/83– Jefferson, NC : McFarland & Company, Inc., Publishers

   Editors: 1982/83– , Sanford Berman and James P. Danky
   Illustrators: 1984/85–1986/87, Jackie Urbanovic; 1988/89, Bert Dodson, Luna
   Ticks, bulbul, Joe Grant, Jim Buckett, Paul Hass.
   1982/83 edition published by Oryx Press.
   "Special Features": 1984/85, The South African connection; 1986/87, The
   Central American/Nicaraguan connection; 1988/89, The Arab connection;
   1990/91, The Columbus Centenary; 1992/93, Sex, censorship, and H. W. Wilson.
   PARTIAL CONTENTS: Work.— Women.— Nukes/peace.—Censorship/
   human rights.— Alternatives.— Service/advocacy/empowerment.— Kids.—
   A/V.— Books and reading.— Just for fun.

   1. Library science. 2. Libraries. 3. Censorship. 4. Librarians—Social
   responsibility. 5. Alternative press. 6. Women librarians. 7. Children's
   library services. 8. Audiovisual library service. 9. Women's library services.
   10. Disabled persons' library services. 11. Minority library services.
   12. Libraries and nuclear warfare. 13. Teenagers' library services. 14. Library
   humor. 15. Apartheid. 16. Anti-Apartheid movement. 17. Libraries—
   Nicaragua. 18. Central America—Bibliography. 19. Anti-Arabism. 20. Columbus
   Quincentenary, 1992-1993. I. Berman, Sanford, 1933- editor. II. Danky, James P.,
   1947- editor.

Figure 7.2   Alternative Cataloguing-in-Publication Data for Berman and Danky's *Alternative Library Literature, 1992/1993: a biennial anthology*

The most striking difference between the two records is in their length. Even before we arrive at the subject headings, Berman's analytical cataloguing has provided far more than the title and editor access points of the Library of Congress's CIP data. He has recognized the intellectual input of all the illustrators of the series and made reference to the special features of each volume, where a single topic is examined in depth outwith the regular sections. These regular sections are provided for in a contents note that uses the headings themselves. Moving to the subject headings we note that Berman's ACIP record has 20 against LC's five. The latter define all contributions as a subdivision of a main

LC subject heading (the subdivision 'Addresses, essays, lectures'), whereas Berman considers the topics in the series as comprehensive topics in their own right, not simply as 'literary' aspects of the topics. He uses language taken from the documents themselves to describe these – 'Alternative press' not LCSH's 'Underground press'; 'Librarians – social responsibility' not 'Librarians and society'; 'Women librarians' not 'Women in library science'. The results are access points far more precise and meaningful than those adopted by LC.

The previous three examples of subject headings are at least represented – however vaguely and unsatisfactorily – by LCSH. There are, however, hundreds of subject headings that Berman has derived from other publications that are not represented at all by LCSH: in the title at hand, headings such as 'Anti-apartheid' and 'Anti-Arabism'. It is from the literature of social change – that is, the alternative literature of its age – that such subjects arise. With them arises the necessity to provide subject access to them in the language they use. To the extent that this language will tend to come from popular movements it is important that such headings that may be sought reflect that language. Not only do the majority of Berman's headings not appear in LC's CIP record, many do not even have an analogue in LCSH. The indexers at LC prefer to wait until the language of such novel subjects becomes standard and is incorporated into the mainstream; until literary warrant (in practice, the adoption of the term in mainstream literature) determines the choice of subject headings. Years after it had become a significant word in the lexicon of music and youth culture, the word 'rave' finally entered LCSH in 1995. But it took the publication of an academic work (Steve Redhead's *Rave off: politics and deviance in contemporary youth culture*) to influence the librarians who compile the subject headings. Yet years earlier the word was in common usage in independent music papers (there was for a time a magazine called *Rave*) and even in *Police Review*. Yet the word is not allowed to stand on its own, neither is it part of the common phrase 'rave scene'; instead the phrase 'rave culture' has been constructed, as befits the recognition of the term from a sociological, rather than a popular, perspective.

These indexers are hardly alone in this practice; too many compilers of thesauri put off incorporating novel terms until usage has 'settled down' and become orthodox. The consequences of such a practice are that new ideas and approaches remain inaccessible through lack of access points or they are buried under unsympathetic or misleading headings. To forestall the entry of such language into the dominant lexicon is to dilute not only the meaning of the words but the importance of the ideas such words portray. It is to marginalize them even further than they are marginalized already, by denying even their semantic traces to be found. The document that is not amenable to the standard indexers' lexicon is a document lost, and thus a set of ideas lost.

Some will protest that until the language is part of the mainstream it should not be incorporated into mainstream indexes and thesauri, lest it proves to be no more than a 'passing phase', requiring emendation or deletion in the future. As with Berman's exhaustive ACIP data, surely librarians have a duty to provide access to ideas and information as they appear and not to sideline them until they become mainstream – if they ever do. Furthermore, if we are to wait until new ideas and their vocabulary are adopted by the mainstream, we will find that such an acceptance tends to be accompanied by a fundamental shift of meaning, what Dorfman and Mattelart name 'recuperation', where a novel idea or phenomenon (we may call it radical, progressive, even threatening) is adopted by the mainstream or significant interests in the mainstream such as government or business 'in such a way that it serves to justify the continued need of the social system and its values'.[3] Consider how 'green', once a progressive term used specifically by radical environmentalists has now been universally adopted, most conspicuously by the business interest, where it usually refers to a public relations exercise that has little to do with environmentalism, such as the promotion of cardboard packaging as 'green'. Until such time as an index or thesaurus incorporated such a term, those seeking information on green issues needed to look under such a scientific and emphatically undemotic term as 'ecology', only relatively recently widely heard. If we are to wait until such ideas are 'recuperated', then we run the risk of providing access only to their vocabulary, which now denotes matters far different from their original conception.

In short, by utilizing the vocabulary of the document, the words of its writers and the culture that has engendered it, an approach such as Berman's provides an accurate and representative account of the ideas of the document, however new or unfamiliar they might be. It provides us with a model for producing catalogue records that will be more meaningful for the user of alternative literature and helps us address many of the problems that cataloguing alternative literature might otherwise bring.

The problems of classification

The classification of alternative publications is no less problematic and equally subject to the limits of the mainstream. Perspectives that examine a subject from more than a single standpoint cannot easily find a useful place in classification schemes that consider such areas of human endeavour as politics, social relations, education and science as essentially discrete. Short of revising the entire philosophy on which their schedules are based, the classifier can do little more than make added entries for all aspects of the topic. As with cataloguing, one might expect to do this with alternative publications somewhat more frequently than with many mainstream publications.

Inadequate CIP data

The number of alternative publications misclassified in CIP data is remarkable. This is not always a result of the novelty of the subject. Noam Chomsky's *Chronicles of dissent*, a collection of interviews dealing with US domestic and foreign policy, is classified by LC at 410.92, as a work about a linguist. One assumes this is because Chomsky is known primarily in the mainstream world as a linguist. Clearly no attempt has been made to examine the contents of the book. The British National Bibliography classifies it at 081, as an American collection of interviews. A more appropriate number than either of these would be 320.973 (US politics). Richard Kadrey's *Covert culture sourcebook* is lazily classified in its CIP data at 306 (Culture and institutions), ignoring the status primarily as a buyer's catalogue of alternative resources (it includes prices and addresses). Whatever sociological import the book may have, it is only as an indirect corollary to this primary function. This error is exacerbated by the classification of Kadrey's second title in the series, *Covert culture sourcebook 2.0* at 306.1 (Subcultures). By contrast *The Millenium Whole Earth Catalog* is classified closely at 380.10296 (Catalogues of appropriate technology), a classification that was more or less appropriate for its first incarnation as *The Last Whole Earth Catalog* back in 1971. The coverage of the catalogue has expanded so much in the ensuing decades that appropriate technology now features on a mere three pages out of a total of almost 400.

Subjects not enumerated in classification schedules

Many subjects are not explicitly enumerated in a classification schedule, leading to inconsistency between CIP records and sowing confusion in the classifier's mind. Such a subject is the Situationists, which have been classified by the British National Bibliography in at least five different parts of the DDC schedules. Some of these locations are understandable: the choice of 700.9045 certainly gives due acknowledgement to the artistic significance of the Situationists, though the -045 subdivision denoting the 1950s is less useful. Simon Ford's forthcoming bibliography has been placed at 016.7009045, although it will cover far more than simply the art of the Situationists. The classifier who chose 322.42094 (European revolutionary and subversive political action groups) comes closer to a more appropriate general number, whilst a location of 941.085 British history, 1945– for *An endless adventure ... an endless passion ... an endless banquet: a situationist scrapbook* is quite misleading and far too general. Perhaps the most sympathetic location, although still very general, is 306 (Culture and institutions) for Sadie Plant's *The most radical gesture.*[4] Implicit in this number is the cultural (artistic) and social significance of the Situationists; DDC's order of precedence also ensures that, this number falling first in the schedules out of all the others used (excepting 016 – Bibliographies as a special case), all other numbers are implicit in it.

Novel, unenumerated subjects must be considered with great care, in order to avoid such discrepancies as these. Before classification takes place, the documents themselves and other sources should be carefully consulted to gauge the actual – rather than the perceived – nature of the intellectual content. Authority files should be maintained as scrupulously as they clearly need to be for subject indexing. As already noted, added entries should also be carefully considered and employed.

'Complementary' classification

A work of alternative literature might well approach a subject in an unexpected way. The classifier's first reaction might well be to place it in a part of the schedules that in effect separates it from the works upon which it comments. By considering the content of alternative titles as complementary to, rather than separate from the mainstream stock, the librarian can ensure that such items will be found adjacent to the items which they comment on or complement. Consider Martin Sprouse's anthology *Sabotage in the American workplace: anecdotes of dissatisfaction, mischief and revenge* and Victor Santoro's *Fighting back on the job*. These might appear to be works dealing with industrial sabotage, for which a number exists in DDC20 (331.893). But they are essentially texts that criticize the traditional hierarchical relationship between employer and employee, aiming to empower the latter. As such they might more valuably be placed at 658.314 (Motivation, morale, discipline) since they deal with dissatisfaction of employees. Similarly, Joyce Nelson's *Sultans of sleaze: public relations and the media* might usefully be read by those studying or investigating the practice of public relations and classified at 659.2 (Public relations; with added entries made under 302.23 (Media) and 388.4730223 (the media as an industry). Although seen as sociopolitical action or 'cultural jamming', the Billboard Liberation Front's *The art and science of billboard improvement* could profitably be located with a collection's main stock on bill-board advertising, to provide a glimpse into the possible at 659.1342 (Outdoor advertising; with an added entry at 302.23). There is no reason why Carl Deal's *The Greenpeace guide to anti-environmental organizations* (Berkeley, Calif.: Odonian, 1993) should not be located with all the other American directories of the environment at 333.702573. This approach might be taken a step further, subverting the original intention of a classification mark (and its attendant vocabulary) by exposing its implicit bias. A title dealing with how the US achieves its foreign policy goals through international aggression might be revealingly located at 303.6250973 Terrorism – United States. This would enable the reader to make instructive comparisons between what Chomsky has called the limited 'retail terrorism' of such groups as the IRA and the PLO and the 'wholesale terrorism' (the invasion of other countries) of world powers such as the US and the former Soviet Union.

Publicizing alternative literature

If we are to exploit our collections of alternative literature fully, we must also ensure that everyone likely to want to make use of them gets to hear of them. Any publicity should always be appropriate to the audience; alternative literature may bring its own idiosyncrasies to bear on this. Put simply, there are two audiences we should expect to attract. The first will comprise people already conversant to some extent with the issues dis-cussed in alternative publications and the nature of these works. These people may hardly be catered for by mainstream library provision and will require special advocacy and outreach activi-ties. We have already noted that networking with local groups and organizations that are themselves responsible for publishing and disseminating alternative literature is an important part of developing our awareness and our collections of alternative lit-erature. Since such people have normally set up their own channels of distribution and methods of acquisition and collection in the absence of any such initiatives by local public or academic libraries, these people are an obvious user group to target in any publicity. Since they are already involved or knowledgeable about the issues and nature of the publications, such publicity may be straightforward enough, requiring little explanation beyond the extent of the collection being acquired and ongoing collection development strategies.

The second audience will comprise those quite unfamiliar with the notion of alternative literature. They might not only be unaware of the interest it might hold for them, they might be wary of it, especially if the mainstream media has done its job well, inculcating people with the belief that anything beyond the mainstream is 'extremist', 'weird' or – equally suspect – 'political'. Since such people will normally be existing library users we can use the library itself as the focus for information and displays about the new collection. In his article 'Organising an Alternative Press Display for Local Libraries',[5] Jason McQuinn provides a model of how this might be achieved. He describes his experiences in setting up and circulating a display of 50 alternative periodicals around his local libraries in Columbia, Missouri. His twin aims were to introduce library users 'to alternative materials they might otherwise never see', at the same time hoping that 'librarians would be forced to confront the question of why, for the most part, these materials aren't in their collections'. McQuinn produced handouts to accompany the display 'listing complete subscription information for all the periodicals'. The centrepiece of the display was a sign listing 'Questions to Think About'. (See Figure 7.3)

McQuinn's display was housed in libraries that did not acquire alternative literature as a matter of course, and therefore such questions were as provocative to the staff as they were intended to be to the users. At this stage heightening awareness and beginning to educate staff and users in the value of alternative publications must begin by asking questions.

Such questions might make people feel uncomfortable, but it is only by exposing people to these titles and by encouraging them to think about them for themselves that alternative litera-

How many of these periodicals have you ever heard of before?

How many of them have you ever seen?

How many of them have you heard of, but never had a chance to see?

How many of them do you think other people (who won't see this display) will ever see or hear of?

Why are so few of these periodicals available in local libraries?

Why are so few of them available in local bookshops and newsagents?

Is there a 'conspiracy of silence' in mainstream institutions and media concerning the alternative press?

Whose interests do alternative publications usually challenge?

Whose interests do they champion?

Who owns the mainstream media?

Who owns the major bookstore chains?

Who controls library budgets and acquisitions by libraries?

Figure 7.3   Questions to think about

ture can begin to find a place in our libraries. The seminars run by the author to promote alternative literature in libraries have all begun with a certain level of disbelief that so much literature could remain unknown by librarians and of distrust that such literature could possibly have anything more to say than is already heard through more mainstream channels. These seminars tend to follow the structure of this book, examining not only what alternative literature is and its concerns, but looking critically at the mainstream media and the dominant selection tools employed by librarians. This is not done in a confrontational manner; rather participants are encouraged to discuss these issues for themselves. Staff training that involves the exploration of such themes through discussion and techniques of critical thinking would be invaluable; such techniques might even be transferred to the users, through lunchtime or evening discussion groups about how the library selects materials and makes it available.

Some might consider that the advocacy of alternative literature is nothing more than a political act. In truth it is a political act, just as a library collection that maintains the status quo whilst excluding alternative literature is a political act. It is unfortunate that the adjective 'political' is normally used pejoratively, when in fact it is utterly neutral. A 'political act' can just as easily be for the better as it can be for the worse; advocating alternative literature in order to extend the range of our library's collections and to improve access to information and ideas for our users is one such act.

References

1. 'Address to New Librarians', *Librarians at Liberty* **1**(2), January 1994, p. 10.
2. Sanford Berman, 'Access to alternatives: new approaches in cataloging', in *Alternative materials in libraries*, edited by James P. Danky and Elliott Shore (Metuchen, NJ and London: Scarecrow Press, 1982), pp. 31–66. In addition to this and the other titles cited here, Berman's *Unreal! Hennepin County Library Subject Headings for fictional characters and places* and the bi-monthly *Hennepin County Library Cataloging Bulletin* provide further guidance and examples of his approach.
3. Ariel Dorfman and Armand Mattelart, *How to read Donald Duck: imperialist ideology in the Disney comic* (New York, NY: International General, 1975), p. 56.
4. Sadie Plant, *The most radical gesture: the Situationist International in a postmodern age*, (London: Routledge, 1992).
5. Jason McQuinn, 'Organising an Alternative Press Display for Local Libraries', *Librarians at Liberty* **1**(1), June 1993, pp. 1–3, 6 and reprinted in *Information for Social Change* (1), Winter 1994, pp. 6–9.

Concluding Remarks

It is now time to draw together some of the dominant themes in this attempt to make sense of alternative information. We have examined many familiar tools of bibliography and stock development: catalogues, indexes, review journals, and noted how these might be used in more creative ways than we are sometimes wont to do. We have seen how the adoption of the practices of researchers: examining references and bibliographies, might profit our stock development activities. The detailed examination of all elements of a journal, right down to advertisements and readers' letters, are potential sources of material and leads to other sources of enquiry. There has been much stress on networking, a crucial activity of the alternative press: 'Networkers know that networks exist for all kinds of purposes and networketry (sic) is the sharing of information, ideas and experience, and the realisation of collective possibilities.'[1]

What all these methods point to is an engagement that goes well beyond standard practices such as browsing catalogues and approvals collections. Such methods will perforce be labour-intensive and time-consuming to begin with, but as we become more confident with the material and learn the language, so to speak – we will find this takes us less time and (dare it be said?) becomes an enjoyable activity. These approaches might even inform and improve our methods of selection and acquisition of more mainstream items.

In his Raymond Williams lecture of 1993, John Pilger asked us 'to examine the often hidden agendas of the institutions in which we work. Isn't it time we broke our silence about the media as a means of social control...?'[2] These same questions may also be asked of our libraries. To ensure a comprehensive and non-sectarian collection of material on all subjects requires a social project of great complexity. Yet as people charged with providing public access to knowledge and all shades of opinion, librarians have a social responsibility easily equal to that of the academic, the doctor or the politician. They have the task of providing a democratic society with the information to preserve, even to improve that democracy. They are required to be unbiased and to serve everyone equally. Censorship promotes élitism, the enemy of democracy. Selection should act as a leveller. It should not ignore marginal interests. If they are to work effectively as agents for social and cultural education librarians need to engage in an activism that is largely lacking in the profession.

A profession might be characterized by the presence of individual responsibility, altruistic in motivation. A profession takes its raw material from science and learning, is itself educable, and leads to a practical and definitive end. As such, librarianship is without doubt a profession. But does that leave our profession fully-defined? Russell Bowden, first Vice-President of the International Federation of Library Associations, thinks not. In his address to the conference 'Emerging Democracies and Freedom of Information', he advised that a profession also had social responsibilities. He urged us not merely to be involved in the management, organization and retrieval of information, but to take an active part in its analysis and evaluation, in how it was presented. He reminded his audience of UNESCO's declaration that information is a basic resource of any nation and that access to it is a basic human right. He added: 'Information is not only a national resource, it is also the medium of social communication.'[3]

Russell Bowden's extension of our professional duties is most welcome. It is heartening to see senior figures in the profession espousing such principles as social responsibility. Yet even he had to admit that these principles were 'strangely ignored by the profession'.

We have seen that we are not going to find sources of alternative literature through the use of picking lists, approvals collections and the mainstream review journals that are mostly used to stock our libraries. We need to go further, developing both our notion of social responsibility to our communities and our own skills in identifying and acquiring alternative literature. We need to develop a critical librarianship in order to educate ourselves and our users in what Marshall McLuhan called 'civil defence against media fallout'. Noam Chomsky has echoed this; he talks of undertaking 'courses in intellectual self-defense'. He goes on to say that we cannot expect to get such courses in school. Where, then, will we get them? In providing a truly comprehensive collection librarians have a significant role in fostering such educational interventions.

Yet such interventions may well be met with opposition. Many who attempt it find themselves isolated or ignored; at worst they are ridiculed or marginalized in similar fashion to the very literature they are seeking to promote. How ironic that such efforts to increase access to information and knowledge, essentially a popularizing movement, should be seen as something unimportant by some.

Working with alternative publications is not easy: it requires diligence, personal investigation, networking and some good fortune. It may require positive discrimination and special pleading at the outset. Our own attitudes to what needs to be in our libraries may have to be changed, widened immeasurably. Let us not forget, as Charles Willett has said, that we 'should consider all points of view, not just academic or political orthodoxy... These books are our glasnost, our samizdat, our free voice.'[4]

References

1. Institute of Fatuous Research, *Pleas for networketry* (London: Playtime For Ever Press, no date), unpaginated.
2. An abridged version of this lecture was published under the title, 'The brave new media world', *New Statesman and Society*, 11 June 1993, pp. 14–15.
3. Keynote address,'Emerging Democracies and Freedom of Information', International Group of the Library Association, held at Somerville College, Oxford, September 1994, (from notes made by the author).
4. Charles Willett, 'Politically controversial monographs: roles of publishers, distributors, booksellers, *Choice* magazine, and librarians in acquiring them for academic libraries', *Building on the first century: proceedings of the Fifth National Conference of the Association of College and Research Libraries*, Cincinnati, Ohio, April 5–8, 1989, Association of College and Research Libraries, 1989, pp. 238–41.

Alternative Resources Mentioned in the Text

Periodicals

3W, 13 Brett Road, London, E8 1JP, England

Access: the supplementary guide to periodicals, John Gordon Burke, PO Box 1492, Evanston, IL 60204–1492, USA

Adbusters Quarterly, The Media Foundation, 1243 West 7th Avenue, Vancouver, BC, V6H 1B7, Canada

Alien Underground, BM Jed, London, WC1N 3XX, England

Alphabet Threat, 3018 J Street #140, Sacramento, CA 95816, USA

Alternative Press Index, Alternative Press Center, PO Box 33109, Baltimore, Maryland 21218, USA

Alternative Press Review, C.A.L. Press, POB 1446, Columbia, MO 65205–1446, USA

Amnesty, Amnesty International, 99–119 Rosebery Avenue, London, EC1R 4RE, England

Anarchist Year Book, Phoenix Press, PO Box 824, London, N1 9DL, England

Anarchy: a journal of desire armed, C.A.L. Press, POB 1446, Columbia, MO 65205–1446, USA

An Camcheachta (*The Starry Plough*), 44 Parnell Square, Dublin 1, Ireland

An Phoblacht (*Republican News*), 58 Parnell Square, Dublin 1, Ireland

Anti-copyright Catalogue, PO Box 368, Cardiff, CF2 1SQ, Wales

Arts Censorship Project Newsletter, 132 West 43rd Street, New York, NY 10036, USA

Baby Sue, PO Box 111, Decatur, GA 30031–1111, USA

Bankcheck Quarterly, International Rivers Network, 1847 Berkeley Way, Berkeley, California, 94703 USA

Bibliozine, John Held Jr, Modern Realism Archive, 1903 McMillan Avenue, Dallas, Texas 75206, USA

Black Flag, BM Hurricane, London, WCN 3XX, England

The Blast!, PO Box 7075, Minneapolis, Minnesota, MN 55407, USA

Bogg: an Anglo-American journal, John Elsberg, 422 North Cleveland St, Arlington, VA 22201, USA and George Cairncross, 31 Belle Vue St, Filey, YO14 9HU, England

bOING bOING, 544 Second Street, San Francisco, CA 94107, USA

The Bug, Box Bug, 46 Denbigh Street, London, SW1, England

Burning Fuse, c/o UK IWW Organising Committee, Secular Hall, 75 Humberstone Gate, Leicester, LE4 5PD, England

Bypass, PO Box 61, Wallasey, Merseyside, L44 8HZ, England

Caduceus, c/o Al Billings, PO Box 1972, Seattle, WA 98111–1972, USA

Casablanca, 31 Clerkenwell Close, London, EC1R 0AT, England

Clean Slate, Centre for Alternative Technology, Machynlleth, Powys, SY20 9AZ, Wales

Contemporary Social Issues, Reference & Research Services, 511 Lincoln Street, Santa Cruz, CA 95060, USA

Contraflow, 56a Infoshop, 56 Crampton Street, London, SE17, England

Counter Information, c/o Transmission, 28 King Street, Glasgow, G1 5QP, Scotland

Counterpoise, c/o Information for Social Change and CRISES Press (see addresses below)

CovertAction Quarterly, 1500 Massachusetts Avenue #732, Washington, D.C. 20005, USA

CultureWatch: a monthly annotated bibliography on culture, art and political affairs, The DataCenter, 464 19th St, Oakland, CA 94612–2297, USA

CVS Bulletin, Suite 115, 6370 York Road, Parma Heights, OH 44130, USA. Copies also available from Mark Pawson (see below).

Dishwasher, PO Box 4827, Arcata, CA 95521, USA

Dissent, 521 Fifth Avenue, New York, NY 10017, USA

DJ, Orpheus Publications, 4th Floor, Centro House, Mandela Street, London, NW1 0DU, England

dreamtime talkingmail, xeoxial endarchy, Rt. 1 Box 131, Lafarge, WI 54639, USA

Earth First! Journal, POB 1415, Eugene, Oregon 97440 USA

East Timor: it's time to talk, British Coalition for East Timor, PO Box 2349, London, E1 3HX, England

EIDOS, PO Box 96, Boston, MA 02137–0096, USA

EIF News, The Environment Council, 21 Elizabeth Street, London, SW1W 9RP, England

Ethical Consumer, Ethical Consumer Research Association, 16 Nicholas Street, Manchester, M1 4EJ, England

Extra!, FAIR (Fairness and Accuracy in Reporting), 130 West 25th Street, New York, NY 10001, USA

Factsheet 5, PO Box 170099, San Francisco, CA 94117–0099, USA

Fatuous Times, BM Jed, London, WC1N 3XX, England

Feminist collections: a quarterly of women's studies resources, Women's Studies Librarian at the University of Wisconsin, 430 Memorial Library, 728 State Street, Madison, Wisconsin 53706, USA

Feminist periodicals: a current listing of contents, address as previous

Fifth Estate, 4632 Second Avenue, Detroit, Wayne County, Michigan 48201, USA

Fire in the mind, PO Box 1706, Knoxville, TN 37901, USA

Flatland, PO Box 2420, Fort Bragg, CA 95437–2420, USA

Fortean Times, John Brown Publishing Ltd, The Boathouse, Crabtree Lane, London, SW6 6LU, England

Fourth World Review, 24 Abercorn Place, London, NW8 9XP, England

Freedom, Freedom Press, 84b Whitechapel High Street, London, E1 7QX, England

Gay Scotland, Calosa Publishing, 58A Broughton Street, Edinburgh, EH1 3SA, Scotland

Gay Times, Millivres Ltd, Ground Floor 5, 116–134 Bayham Street, Worldwide House, London, NW1 0BA, England

Global Mail, PO Box 597996, Chicago, IL 60659, USA

Green Anarchist, PO Box 407, Camberley, GU15 3FL, England

Greenline, PO Box 5, Lostwithiel, Cornwall, PL22 0YT, England

Grim Humour, PO Box 63, Herne Bay, Kent, CT6 6YU, England

Heavy Flow, No-tell Motel, (GFR) 25 Eyre Place, Edinburgh, EH3 5EX, Scotland

Hennepin County Library Cataloging Bulletin, Hennepin County Library, 12601 Ridgedale Drive, Minnetonka, MN 55305–1909, USA

Here and Now, c/o Transmission, 28 King Street, Glasgow, G1 5QP, Scotland

Holy Titclamps, PO Box 590488, San Francisco, CA 94159–0488, USA

The Idler, 51 St Stephen's Gardens, London, W2, England

In These Times, Institute for Public Affairs, 2040 N. Milwaukee Avenue, Chicago, IL 60647, USA

Index on Censorship, Writers and Scholars International, Lancaster House, 33 Islington High Street, London, N1 9LH, England

Industrial Worker, 1095 Market Street #204, San Franscisco, CA 94103, USA

Indy, Blackmore Publishing, 6281 S. Dolphin Drive, Floral City, FL 34436, USA

Information for Social Change, 14 Hugh Miller Place, Edinburgh, EH3 5JG, Scotland

International Newsletter, Amnesty International, 99–119 Rosebery Avenue, London, EC1R 4RE, England

KSL, BM Hurricane, London, WC1 3XX, England

The Left Index, Reference & Research Services, 511 Lincoln Street, Santa Cruz, CA 95060, USA

The Lesbian Review of Books, PO Box 6369, Altadena, CA 91003–6369, USA

LibED, Phoenix House, 170 Wells Road, Bristol, BS4 2SG, England

Libertarian Labor Review, PO Box 2824, Champaign, IL 61825, USA

Librarians at Liberty, CRISES Press, 1716 SW Williston Road, Gainesville, FL 32608, USA

Light's List, Photon Press, 29 Longfield Road, Tring, Hertfordshire, HP23 4DG, England

Lobster, Robin Ramsay, 214 Westbourne Avenue, Hull, HU5 3JB, England and Steve Dorril, 135 School Street, Netherthong, Holmfirth, HD7 2YB, England

Magonia, John Rimmer, John Dee Cottage, 5 James Terrace, Mortlake Churchyard, London, SW14 8HB, England

The Match!, PO Box 3488, Tucson, AZ 85722, USA

Maximumrockandroll, PO Box 460760, San Francisco, CA 94146–0760, USA

The Message, 7 Primrose Road, Halton, Leeds, LS15 7RS, England

MFTEQ, PO Box 87, Ilford, Essex, IG1 3HJ, England

Mixmag, PO Box 89, London, W14 8ZW, England

The Morning Star, 1–3 Ardleigh Road, N1 4HS, England

Mother Jones, 1663 Mission Street, San Francisco, CA 94103, USA

MSRRT Newsletter, Chris Dodge, 4645 Columbus Avenue South, Minneapolis, MN 55407, USA

The Nation, 72 Fifth Avenue, New York, NY 10011, USA

NCFE Bulletin, 1402 3rd Avenue, #421, Seattle, WA 98101, USA

ND, PO Box 4144, Austin, Texas 78765, USA

Neon News, Ted Prisig, PO Box 668, Volcano, HI 96785, USA

New Anarchist Review, c/o 84b Whitechapel High Street, London, E1 7QX, England

New Hope International, Gerald England, 20 Werneth Avenue, Gee Cross, Hyde, Cheshire, SK14 5NL, England

New Internationalist, PO Box 79, Hertford, SG14 1AQ, England

New pages: alternatives in print & media, New Pages Press, Box 438, Grand Blanc, MI 48439, USA

The Newsline, BCM Box 747, London, WC1N 3XX, England

New Statesman and Society, Foundation House, Perseverance Works, 38 Kingsland Road, London, E2 8DQ, England

NO LONGER A FANzine, Joseph A. Gervasi, 142 Frankford Avenue, Blackwood, NJ 08012, USA

Obscure, POB 1334, Milwaukee, Wisconsin 53201, USA

Open Eye, BM Open Eye, London, WC1N 3XX, England

Open Magazine Pamphlet Series, PO Box 2726, Westfield, New Jersey 07091, USA

Paranoia, PO Box 3570, Cranston, RI 02910, USA

Peace News , 5 Caledonian Road, London, N1 9DX, England

The Pink Paper, 77 Garden City Row, London, N1 8EZ, England

Planet News, 87 Kirkstall Road, London, SW2 4HE, England

Planetary Connections, PO Box 44, Evesham, Worcestershire, WR12 7YW, England

Practical Anarchy, PO Box 179, College Park, MD 20741–1079, USA

Private Eye, Pressdram, 6 Carlisle Street, London, W1V 5RG, England

The Progressive, 409 East Main Street, Madison, WI 53703, USA

Progressive Librarian, Box 2203, Times Square Station, New York, NY 10108, USA

Proletarian Gob, Folder 19, 30 Silver Street, Reading, RG1, England

Promises and Disappointments, Kevin McClure, 42 Victoria Road, Mount Charles, St Austell, Cornwall, PL25 4QD, England

Propaganda Review, c/o Media Alliance, Building D, Fort Mason Center, San Francisco, CA 94123, USA

Queer Zine Explosion, PO Box 590488, San Francisco, CA 94159–0488, USA

Qz, Alleged Literature, c/o Jeremy Dennis, 26 Princes Street, Oxford, OX4 1DD, England

The Raven, Freedom Press, 84b Whitechapel High Street, London, E1 7QX, England

Red Pepper, 3 Gunthorpe Street, London, E1 7RP, England

Republican News, 58 Parnell Square, Dublin 1, Ireland

Revisionist Researcher, PO Box 236, Dresden, New York 14441, USA

Rouge, BM Rouge, London, WC1N 3XX, England

Secrets, Campaign for Freedom of Information, 88 Old Street, London, EC1V 9AR, England

Short circuit, PO Box 70, Bayside, NY 11361, USA

Sipapu, Noel Peattie, 23311 County Road 88, Winters, CA 9564 USA

Small Press, Kymbolde Way, Wakefield, RI 02879, USA

Small Press Book Review, Greenfield Press, PO Box 176, Southport, CT 06490, USA

Small Press News, Stony Hills Productions, Box 780-H, Weeks Mills, New Sharon, ME 04955, USA

Small Press Review (incorporating *Small Magazine Review*), Dustbooks, PO Box 100, Paradise, CA 95967, USA

Social Theory, Reference & Research Services, 511 Lincoln Street, Santa Cruz, CA 95060, USA

Society and Nature, PO Box 637, Littleton, CO 80160–0637, USA

The Starry Plough, 44 Parnell Square, Dublin 1, Ireland

Statewatch, PO Box 1516, London, N16 0EW, England

Steamshovel Press, POB 23715, St Louis, MO 63121, USA

The Steward, Rick Barnes, PO Box 250224, San Francisco, CA 94125, USA

The Stockbridge and Newtown Rocket, c/o The Peace and Justice Centre, St John's Church, Princes Street, Edinburgh, EH2, Scotland

Taproot Reviews: news and reviews from the micropress underground, PO Box 585, Lakewood, OH 44107, USA

Third World Resources, Data Center, 464 19th Street, Oakland, CA 94612, USA

This Magazine, 16 Skey Lane, Toronto, Ontario, M6J 3S4, Canada

TRANET , PO Box 567, Rangeley, ME 04970, USA

Troops Out, BM TOM, London, WC1N 3XX, England

Trotwatch, c/o Box NDF, 72 Radford Road, Hyson Green, Nottingham, NG7 5FT, England

U-Direct, Mary Kuntz Press, PO Box 476617, Chicago, Illinois 60647, USA

Unclassified, Verne Lyon, 921 Pleasant Street, Des Moines, IA 50309, USA

Underground, PO Box 3285, London, SW2 3NN, England

The Underground and Alternative Press in Britain during [year], Research Publications, PO Box 45, Reading, RG1 8HF, England

Unschooling Ourselves, Lowry House Publishers, POB 1014, Eugene, Oregon 97440–1014, USA

Utne Reader, PO Box 1974, Marion, OH 43306–2074, USA

Vague, BCM Box 7207, London, WC1N 3XX, England

Whole Earth Review, 27 Gate Five Road, Sausalito, CA 94965, USA
Why..?, 77 Heald Place, Rusholme, Manchester, MI4 4AQ, England
Wild Earth, POB 455, Richmond, VT 05477, USA
Wired, PO Box 191826, San Francisco, CA 94119–1826, USA and Freepost TN 7268, PO Box 101, Hastings, TN35 4BR, England
Z Magazine, 116 St Botolph Street, Boston, MA 02115, USA
Zum!, 40 Marmion Road, Liverpool, L17 8TX, England

Books and pamphlets

Alternative Library Literature, edited by Sanford Berman and James Danky, Jefferson, North Carolina: McFarland, 1994.

Alternative materials in libraries, edited by James P. Danky and Elliott Shore, Metuchen, New Jersey: Scarecrow Press, 1982.

Alternative publications: a guide to directories, bibliographies and other sources, edited by Cathy Seitz Whitaker, Jefferson, North Carolina: McFarland, 1990.

Alternative publishers of books in North America, compiled by Byron Anderson, 2nd ed., Gainesville, Florida: CRISES Press, 1995.

Alternatives in print: an international catalog of books, pamphlets, periodicals and audiovisual materials, compiled by the Task Force on Alternatives in Print, Social Responsibilities Round Table, American Library Association, 6th ed., New York, NY: Neal-Schuman; London: Mansell, 1980.

APT for Libraries: Alternative Press Titles for the General Reader, edited by Charles Willett, Gainesville, Florida: CRISES Press.

The Arms Traders, London: Campaign Against Arms Trade, 1992.

The artist publisher: a survey by Coracle Press, London: Crafts Council, 1986.

Barsamian, David, *Stenographers to power: media and propaganda,* Monroe, Maine: Common Courage, 1992.

Berman, Sanford, *Prejudices and antipathies: a tract on the LC Subject Heads concerning people,* Jefferson, North Carolina: McFarland, 1993.

Berman, Sanford, *Unreal! Hennepin County Library Subject Headings for fictional characters and places*, 2nd ed., Jefferson, North Carolina: McFarland, 1992.

Berman, Sanford, *Worth noting: editorials, letters, essays, an interview and bibliography*, Jefferson, North Carolina: McFarland, 1988.

Billboard Liberation Front, *The art and science of billboard improvement*, San Francisco, California: Los Cabrones, 1990.

Black, Bob, *The abolition of work*, New York, New York: Feh! Press, [no date].

Black, Bob, *The abolition of work*, Sheffield: Pirate Press, 1990.

Black, Bob, *The abolition of work and other essays*, Port Townshend, Washington: Loompanics Unlimited, [1986].

Black, Bob, *Beneath the underground*, Portland, Oregon: Feral House, 1994.

Blazwick, Iwona, *An endless adventure ... an endless passion ... an endless banquet: a situationist scrapbook: the Situationist International selected documents from 1957 to 1962: documents tracing the impact on British culture from the 1960s to the 1980s*, London:ICA/Verso, 1989.

Book your own fuckin' life: do it yourself resource guide, Cicero, Illinois: Maximumrocknroll/Rocco Publishing, [1993?].

Censored!: the news that didn't make the news ... and why, New York, New York: Four Walls and Eight Windows.

Chomsky, Noam, *Chronicles of Dissent: interviews with David Barsamian*, Monroe, Maine: Common Courage and Edinburgh: AK, 1992.

Chomsky, Noam, *Keeping the rabble in line: interviews with David Barsamian*, Edinburgh: AK Press, 1994.

Chomsky, Noam, *Letters from Lexington: reflections on propaganda*, Monroe, Maine: Common Courage and Edinburgh: AK, 1993.

Chomsky, Noam, *Media control: the spectacular achievements of propaganda*,Westfield, New Jersey: Open Magazine Pamphlet Series, 1992.

Chomsky, Noam, *Necessary illusions: thought control in democratic societies*, London: Pluto Press, 1989.

Chomsky, Noam, *What Uncle Sam really wants*, Berkeley, California: Odonian Press, 1992.

Curtis, Liz. *Ireland: the propaganda war: the media and the 'battle for hearts and minds'*, London: Pluto Press, 1984.

Deal, Carl, *The Greenpeace guide to anti-environmental organisations*, Berkeley, California: Odonian Press, 1987.

Dear motorist . . . the social ideology of the motor car, Oxford: Insitute of Social Disengineering, [no date].

Debord, Guy, *Society of the spectacle*, Detroit, Michigan: Black and Red, 1983.

Demolish serious buildings, London: Playtime For Ever Press, [no date].

Dery, Mark, *Culture jamming: hacking, slashing and sniping in the empire of signs*, Westfield, New Jersey: Open Magazine Pamphlet Series, 1993.

Diggers and Dreamers: the guide to communal living, edited by Chris Coates and others, Winslow: Communes Network, 1993.

Directory of Intentional Communities: a guide to co-operative living, Louisa, Virginia: Directory of Intentional Communities.

Directory of Libertarian Periodicals, Buffalo, New York: Jim Stumm.

Directory of Poetry Publishers, edited by Len Fulton, Paradise, California: Dustbooks.

Dodge, Chris, *A zine-ography*, Minneapolis: Chris Dodge, 1995.

Dorfman, Ariel and Mattelart, Armand, *How to read Donald Duck: imperialist ideology in the Disney comic*, New York, New York: International General, 1975.

Erler, Bob, *Anarchist Booklist*, New York, New York: Libertarian Book Club, 1993.

Field guide to alternative media: a directory to reference and selection tools useful in accessing small and alternative press publications and independently produced media, edited and compiled by Patricia J. Case, Chicago, Illinois: Task Force on Alternatives in Print, Social Responsibilities Round Table, American Library Association, 1984.

Flyposter frenzy: posters from the Anticopyright Network, edited by Matthew Fuller, London: Working Press.

Ford, Simon, *The realization and suppression of the Situationist International – an annotated bibliography, 1972–92*, Edinburgh: AK, 1995.

From radical left to extreme right: a bibliography of current periodicals of protest, controversy, advocacy, or dissent, with dispassionate content-summaries to guide librarians and other educators, compiled by Gail Skidmore and Theodore Jurgen Spahn, 3rd ed., Metuchen, New York: Scarecrow, 1987.

Griffin, John, *A Structured Anarchism*, London: Freedom Press, 1991.

Gunderloy, Mike and Janice, and Goldberg, Cari, *The world of zines: a guide to the independent magazine revolution*, New York, New York: Penguin, 1992.

Held, John, *Mail art: an annotated bibliography*, Metuchen, New Jersey: Scarecrow Press, 1991.

The heretic's guide to the bible, [no place of publication]: Irate Press, [no date].

Herman, Edward, *Beyond hypocrisy: decoding the news in an age of propaganda*, Boston, Massachusetts: South End, 1992.

Herman, Edward and Chomksy, Noam, *Manufacturing Consent: the political economy of the mass media*, New York, New York: Pantheon, 1988.

Hoey, Mick, *The alternative press in Britain: a select bibliography*, Brighton: Smoothie, 1973.

Housman's Peace Diary and World Peace Directory, London: Housmans.

Human rights organizations and periodicals directory, Berkeley, California: Meiklejohn Civil Liberties Institute.

Institute of Fatuous Research, *Pleas for networketry*, London: Playtime For Ever Press, [no date].

International directory of little magazines and small presses, edited by Len Fulton, Paradise, California: Dustbooks.

James, Robin, *Cassette mythos*, Brooklyn, New York: Semiotext(e), 1992.

Kadrey, Richard, *Covert culture sourcebook*, New York, New York: St Martin's Press, 1993.

Kadrey, Richard, *Covert culture sourcebook 2.0*, New York, New York: St Martin's Press, 1994.

Lang, Peter, *LETS work: rebuilding the local economy*, Bristol: Worldly Goods, [no date].

Law, Larry, *Spectacular Times*, London: A Distribution, [various dates].

Lee, Martin A., *Unreliable sources: a guide to detecting bias in news media*, New York, New York: Carol Publishing Group, 1990.

Libertarian Education, *Freedom in education: a guide to the liberation of learning*, Bristol: Libertarian Education, 1992.

Llewellyn, Grace, *The teenage liberation handbook: how to quit school and get a real life and education*, Eugene, Oregon: Lowry House Publishers, 1991.

Love and Rage Community Society, *A Deschooling reader: alternatives, analysis and ideas for doing things better*, Vancouver, British Columbia: Love and Rage Community Society, [no date].

Luber, Burkhard, *The World at Your Keyboard: an alternative guide to global computer networking*, Oxford: Jon Carpenter Publishing, 1993.

Lynn, Robert, *Vote: what for?* No publishing details, distributed by AK.

Lyons, Joan, *Artists' books: a critical anthology and sourcebook*, Rochester, New York: Visual Studies Workshop, 1991.

MacLean, Eleanor, *Between the lines: how to detect bias and propaganda in the media and everyday life*, Montreal: Black Rose, 1981.

Macrocosm USA: possibilities for a new progressive era, edited by Sandi Brockway, Cambria, California: Macrocosm USA.

Magazines for Libraries, compiled by Bill and Linda Sternberg Katz, New Providence, New Jersey: Bowker.

Mander, Gerry, *Four Arguments for the Elimination of Television*, New York, New York: Quill, 1978.

Manufacturing consent: Noam Chomsky and the media, edited by Mark Achbar, Montreal: Black Rose Books, 1994.

Martin, Brian, *Strip the experts*, London: Freedom, 1991.

Matiasz, G.A., *End Time*, Edinburgh: AK, 1994.

The millenium whole earth catalog: access to tools and ideas for the twenty-first century, edited by Howard Rheingold, San Francisco, California: HarperSanFrancisco, 1994.

Miller, David, *Don't mention the war: Northern Ireland, propaganda and the media*, London: Pluto Press, 1994.

Milne, Seumas, *The enemy within*, London: Verso, 1993.

Moorish Orthodox Radio Collective, *Radio Sermonettes*, New York, New York: Libertarian Book Club, 1992. (Republished with an introduction as: *Immediatism: essays by Hakim Bey*, Edinburgh and San Francisco: AK, 1994.)

Nelson, Joyce, *Sultans of sleaze: public relations and the media*, Monroe, Maine: Common Courage, 1989.

Oglesby, Carl, *Who killed JFK?*, Berkeley, California: Odonian Press, 1992.

Pawson, Mark , *Eco-Frenzy*, London: Mark Pawson, 1993.

Pawson, Mark, *Mark's Little Book About Kinder Eggs*, London: Mark Pawson, 1989.

Play is everything work is not, London: Playtime For Ever Press, [no date].

Progressive Periodicals Directory, 2nd ed., compiled by Craig T. Canan, Nashville, Tennessee: Progressive Education, 1989.

The Radical Bookseller Directory 1992, compiled by Einde O'Callaghan, London: The Radical Bookseller, 1992.

Rimmer, Steve, *Planet Internet*, New York, New York: Windcrest/McGraw-Hill, 1995.

Rooum, Donald, *What is Anarchism?*, London: Freedom Press, 1993.

Sabotage in the American workplace: anecdotes of dissatisfaction, mischief and revenge, edited by Martin Sprouse, San Francisco, California: Pressure Drop, and Edinburgh: AK, 1992.

Said, Edward, *The pen and the sword: conversations with David Barsamian*, Edinburgh: AK, 1994.

Santoro, Victor, *Fighting back on the job*, Port Townsend, Washington: Loompanics Unlimited, 1984.

Schcheglov, Ivan, *Formulary for a new urbanism*, London: London Psychogeographical Association/Unpopular Books, [no date].

The Scum Directory, Manchester: The Scum Directory.

Shor, Ira, *Critical thinking and everyday life*, Montreal: Black Rose, 1980.

Shotton, John, *No master high or low: libertarian education and schooling in Britain: 1890–1990*, Bristol: Libertarian Education, 1993.

Small press record of books in print, edited by Len Fulton, Paradise, California: Dustbooks.

The Small Press Yearbook, edited by John Nicholson, London: Small Press Group of Britain, 1994.

Small Presses and Little Magazines of the UK and Ireland: an address list, compiled by Peter Finch, 11th ed., Cardiff: Oriel, 1994.

Spring, Joel, *Primer of libertarian education*, Montreal: Black Rose, 1975.

Statewatching the new Europe: a handbook on the European state, London: Statewatch, 1993.

Stockholm International Peace Research Institute Yearbook, Stockholm: Stockholm International Peace Research Institute.

Test card F: television, mythinformation and social control, Edinburgh: AK, 1994.

TV Times: a seven day guide to killing your TV, Oxford: OxFIN, [no date].

Vague, Tom, *The great British mistake: Vague 1977–92*, Edinburgh: AK Press, 1994. (Also known as *Vague 25*)

Vaneigem, Raoul, *The revolution of everyday life*, rev. ed., Seattle, Washington: Left Bank, and London: Rebel Press, 1994.

War and peace in the Balkans: a resource guide to ex-Yugoslavia, 2nd ed., New York, New York: Balkan War Resource Group, 1994.

Ward, Colin, *Anarchy in Action*, London: Freedom Press, 1982.

A Who's Who of the British Secret State, compiled by Steve Dorril, Hull: Lobster, 1989.

World Directory of Minorities, London: Minority Rights Group.

Yates, John, *Stealworks*, Edinburgh: AK, and London: Active Distribution, 1994.

Zepezaur, Mark, *The CIA's greatest hits*, Berkeley, California: Odonian Press, 1994.

Zerowork: The anti-work anthology, edited by Bob Black and Tad Kepley, Brooklyn, New York: Autonomedia, 1993.

Publishers, distributors and organizations

A Distribution, 84b Whitechapel High Street, London, E1 7QX, England

Active Distribution, BM Active, London, WC1N 3XX, England

AK Press and Distribution, 22 Lutton Place, Edinburgh, EH8 9PE, Scotland, and PO Box 40682, San Francisco, CA 94140–0682, USA

Alternative Radio, 2129 Mapleton, Boulder, CO 80304, USA

The Alternative Reading Room, 40 Wall Street, Ashville, North Carolina, NC 28801, USA

American Civil Liberties Union, 132 West 43rd Street, New York, NY 10036, USA

Amnesty International, 99–119 Rosebery Avenue, London, EC1R 4RE, England

Amok, 1764 North Vermont Avenue, Los Angeles, CA 90027, USA

The Anarchist Archives Project, Jerry Kaplan, AA Project, PO Box 1323, Cambridge, MA 02238, USA

Animal Liberation Front, ALF Supporters Group, BCM 1160, London, WC1N 3XX, England

Aporia Press, 308 Camberwell New Road, London, SE5 0RW, England

Arbeitskreis Critische Bibliothekarinnen, c/o Maria Kuhn-Ludewig, Sonnenplatz 14, D-44137 Dortmund, Germany

Archive cassette catalog, Archives on audio, PO Box 170023, San Francisco, California 94117-0023, USA

Atlas Press, BCM Atlas Press, London, WC1N 3XX, England

Autonomedia, POB 568, Brooklyn, NY 11211-0568, USA

Balkan War Resource Group, c/o War Resisters League, 339 Lafayette Street, New York, NY 10012, USA

Black and Red, PO Box 02374, Detroit, Michigan 48202, USA

Black Rose Books, C.P. 1258, Succ. Place du Parc, Montreal, Quebec, H2W 2R3, Canada

British Coalition for East Timor, PO Box 2349, London, E1 3HX, England

Burning Press, PO Box 585, Lakewood, OH 44107, USA

Los Cabrones. No address. Distributed by AK.

Campaign Against Arms Trade, 11 Goodwin Street, London, N4 3HQ, England

Campaign for Freedom of Information, 88 Old Street, London, EC1V 9AR, England

Jon Carpenter Publishing, PO Box 129, Oxford, OX1 4PH, England

The Centre for the Academic Study of Extremes in Human Experience Research Project, POB 28760, Seattle, WA 98118, USA

Centre International de Recherches sur L'Anarchisme, Avenue de Beaumont 24, CH-1012 Lausanne, Switzerland

C. G. H. Services, Cwm Gwen Hall, Pencader, Dyfed, SA39 9HA, Wales

Chthonios Books, 7 Tamarisk Steps, Hastings, Sussex, TN34 3DN, England

Church of the SubGenius, PO Box 140306, Dallas, TX 75214, USA

Civic Media Center and Library, 1021 West University Avenue, Gainesville, Florida 32601, USA

Committee of Small Magazine Editors and Publishers, POB 420703, San Francisco, CA 94142–0703, USA

Common Courage, PO Box 702, Monroe, ME 04951, USA

The Commonweal Collection, c/o J.B. Priestley Library, University of Bradford, Bradford, BD7 1DP, England

Communes Network, c/o Redfield Community, Winslow, Buckinghamshire, MK18 3LZ, England

CommUnity, 89 Mayfair Avenue, Worcester Park, Surrey, KT4 7SJ, England

Computer Professionals for Social Responsibility, PO Box 717, Palo Alto, CA 94302, USA

Copyright Violation Squad, Suite 115, 6370 York Road, Parma Heights, OH 44130, USA

Counter Productions, PO Box 556, London, SE5 0RW, England

Dalkey Archive, 4241 Illinois State University, Normal, IL 61790–4241, USA

Data Center, 464 19th Street, Oakland, CA 94612, USA

Desert Moon Periodicals/Xines, Inc., 1226-A Calle de Comercio, Santa Fe, NM 87501, USA

Directory of Intentional Communities: a guide to co-operative living, Route 4, PO Box 169-NC, Louisa, VA 23093, USA

Dodge, Chris, 4645 Columbus Avenue, Minneapolis, MN 55407, USA

Dustbooks, PO Box 100, Paradise, CA 95967, USA

East Timor Action Network, PO Box 1182, White Plains, New York 10602, USA

Education Otherwise, 110 Cambridge Street, Wolverton, Milton Keynes, MK12 5AH, England

Electronic Frontier Foundation, 1001 G Street NW, Suite 950 E, Washington DC 20001, USA

Environmental Information Forum, The Environment Council, 21 Elizabeth Street, London, SW1W 9RP, England

Exact Change, PO Box 544, Cambridge MA 02139, USA

FAIR (Fairness and Accuracy in Reporting), 130 West 25th Street, New York, NY 10001, USA

Feh! Press, 147 Second Avenue #603, New York, NY 10003, USA

Feral House, PO Box 3466, Portland, OR 97208, USA

Fine Print, 6448 Hwy 290 East, Suite B-104, Austin, TX 78723-1038, USA

Fortean Tomes, John Brown Publishing Ltd, The Boathouse, Crabtree Lane, London, SW6 6LU, England

Four Walls Eight Windows, PO Box 548, Village Station, New York, NY 10014, USA

Freedom Press, 84b Whitechapel High Street, London, E1 7QX, England

Frontline Books, 1 Newton Street, Piccadilly, Manchester, M1 1HW, England

Growing without Schooling, 2269 Massachusetts Avenue, Cambridge, MA 02140, USA

Human Rights Watch, 485 Fifth Avenue, New York, NY 10017, USA and 90 Borough High Street, London, SE1 1LL, England

Human Scale Education, 96 Carlingcott, Nr. Bath, BA2 8AW, England

Indelible Inc, BCM 1698, London, WC1N 3XX, England

Industrial Workers of the World, 1095 Market Street #204, San Francisco, CA 94103, USA and Secular Hall, 75 Humberstone Gate, Leicester, LE4 5PD, England

Information for Social Change, 14 Hugh Miller Place, Edinburgh, EH3 5JG, Scotland

Inland Book Co., PO Box 120261, East Haven, CT 06512, USA

Institute for Historical Review, 1822 1/2 Newport Blvd., Suite 191, Costa Mesa, CA 92627, USA

Institute of Social Disengineering, Box B, 111 Magdalen Road, Oxford, OX4, England

Intermediate Technology Development Group, 103–105 Southampton Row, London, WC1B 4HH, England

International General, POB 350, New York, NY 10013, USA

Irate Press. No address. Distributed by AK.

Kerr, Charles H., 1740 West Greenleaf Avenue, Chicago, Illinois 60626, USA

Left Bank Books, 92 Pike Street, Seattle, WA 98101, USA

Left Bank Distribution, 4142 Brooklyn Avenue NE, Seattle, WA 98105, USA

Libertarian Alliance, 25 Chapter Chambers, Esterbrooke Street, London, SW1P 4NN, England

Libertarian Book Club, 339 Lafayette Street, Room 202, New York City, NY 10012, USA

Libertarian Education, Phoenix House, 170 Wells Road, Bristol, BS4 2AG, England

Library and Information Workers' Organisation, c/o University Library, PO Box 375, Pietermaritzburg 3200, South Africa

London Greenpeace, 5 Caledonian Road, London, N1 9DX, England

London Psychogeographical Association, Box 15, 138 Kingsland High Street, London, E8 2NS, England

Loompanics Unlimited, PO Box 1197, Port Townsend, WA 98368, USA

Love and Rage Community Society,1450 Venables, Vancouver, British Columbia, V5L 2G5, Canada

Lowry House Publishers, POB 1014, Eugene, Oregon 97440–1014, USA

McFarland and Company, Box 611, Jefferson, North Carolina 28640, USA

MACOS (Musicians Against the Copyright of Samples), Rodelheimer Landstrasse 132, D-60487, Frankfurt/Main, Germany

Macrocosm USA, PO Box 185, Cambria, CA 93428–0185, USA

Malice Aforethought Press, 328 Brettenham Road, London, E17 5AU, England

Millivres Books, 33 Bristol Gardens, Brighton, BN2 5JR, England

Minority Rights Group, 379 Brixton Road, London, SW9 7DE, England

Mushroom Bookshop, 10-12 Heathcote Street, Nottingham, NG1 3AA, England

National Campaign for Freedom of Expression, 1402 3rd Avenue, #421, Seattle, WA 98101, USA

National Small Press Centre at Middlesex University, All Saints Site, White Hart Lane, London, N17 8HR, England

New Paradigms Project, c/o A-albionic Research, PO Box 20273, Ferndale, MI 48220, USA

New Society Publishers, 4527 Springfield Avenue, Philadelphia, PA 19143, USA

Odonian Press, Box 32375, Tucson, Arizona, AZ 85751, USA

Open Magazine, PO Box 2726, Westfield, New Jersey 07091, USA

Oriel, The Friary, Cardiff, CF1 4AA, Wales

OxFIN, 21 Cave Street, Oxford, OX4, England

Pantheon, 201 East 50th Street, New York, NY 10012, USA

Paper Tiger Television, 339 Lafayette Street, New York, NY 10012, USA

Pawson, Mark, PO Box 664, London, E3 4QR, England

Perennial Books, PO Box B14, Montague, MA 01351, USA

Phoenix Press, PO Box 824, London, N1 9DL, England

Pike, Derrick A., 1 Market Place, Glastonbury, BA6 9HD, England

Pirate Press, Black Star, PO Box 4346, Sheffield, S1 1NY, England

Play for Life, Advice Arcade, 4 Guildhall Hill, Norwich, NR2 1JH, England

Playtime For Ever Press, BM Jed, London, WC1N 3XX, England

Pluto Press, 345 Archway Road, London, N6 5AA, England

Pressure Drop Press, POB 460754, San Francisco, CA 94146, USA

Printed Matter Bookstore at Dia, 77 Wooster Street, New York, NY 10012, USA

Progressive Education, PO Box 120574, Nashville, TN 37212, USA

Progressive Librarians' Guild, Box 2203, Times Square Station, New York, NY 10108, USA

Public Information Research, POB 5199, Arlington, VA 22205, USA

Quill, PO Box 3109-DB, Harlingen, TX 78551, USA

Radical Booksellers' Network, PO Box 1706, Knoxville, TN 37901, USA

Rebel Press, Box R, 84b Whitechapel High Street, London, E1 7QX, England

Reference & Research Services, 511 Lincoln Street, Santa Cruz, CA 95060, USA

Rocco Publishing, 2427 South 58th St, Cicero, IL 60650, USA

SAF, 12 Conway Gardens, Wembley, Middlesex, HA9 8TR, England

St Martin's Press, 175 Fifth Avenue, New York, NY 10010, USA

Scarecrow Press, PO Box 4167, Metuchen, New Jersey 08840, USA

The Scum Directory, PO Box 155, Manchester, M60 1FT, England

Semiotext(e), POB 568, Brooklyn, NY 11211–0568, USA

Serpent's Tail, 4 Blackstock Mews, London, N4 2BT, England

Kate Sharpley Library and Documentation Centre, BM Hurricane, London, WCN 3XX, England

Silid Aklatan, PO Box 187, North Hollywood, CA 91603, USA

Sinn Fein Book Bureau Catalogue, 44 Parnell Square, Dublin1, Ireland

Small Press Group of Britain, National Small Press Centre at Middlesex University, All Saints Site, White Hart Lane, London, N17 8HR, England

South End Press, 116 Saint Botolph Street, Boston MA 02115, USA

Statewatch, PO Box 1516, London, N16 0EW, England

Stockbridge and New Town Solidarity Network, c/o The Peace and Justice Centre, St John's Church, Princes Street, Edinburgh, EH2, Scotland

Stockholm International Peace Research Institute, Pipers vag 28, 17073 Solna, Sweden

Stumm, Jim, Box 29, Hiler Branch, Buffalo, NY 14223, USA

TAPOL, 111 Northwood Road, Thornton Heath, Surrey, CR7 8HW, England

Turnaround, 27 Horsell Road, London, N5 1XL, England

Unpopular Books, Box 15, 138 Kingsland High Street, London, E8 2NS, England

Verso, 6 Meard Street, London, W1V 3HR, England

West and Wilde Bookshop, 25a Dundas Street, Edinburgh, EH3 6QQ, Scotland

Women's Studies Librarian at the University of Wisconsin, 430 Memorial Library, 728 State Street, Madison, Wisconsin 53706, USA

Working Press, 85 St Agnes Place, Kennington, London, SE11 4BB, England

World Development Movement, 25 Beehive Place, London, SW9 7QR, England

Worldly Goods, 10–12 Picton Street, Montpelier, Bristol, BS6 5QA, England

Worldwide web resources

EnviroWeb – http://envirolink.org

Factsheet 5 Electric –http://kzsu.stanford.edu.uwi/f5e/f5e.html, http://www.well.com

Internet Directory of Published Writers – http://www.bocklabs.wisc.edu/ims/writers.html

Mid-Atlantic Infoshop Home Page – http://www.wam.umd.edu/~ctmunson/Infoshop.html

NativeNet – http://kuhttp.cc.ukans.edu/~marc/native_main.html

New Paradigms Project – WWW: http://gopher.a-albionic.com:9006/

Spunk Press – http://www.cwi.nl/cwi/people/Jack.Jansen/spunk/Spunk_Home.html

Index

195